EDITORIAL RESEARCH REPORTS
ON THE

Trillion-Dollar
Economy

Published by Congressional Quarterly, Inc.
1735 K Street, N.W.
Washington, D.C. 20006

39314

Published July 1970

Library of Congress Catalogue Card Number 78-13195
Standard Book No. 87187-011-8

Editorial Research Reports
Editor Emeritus, Richard M. Boeckel
Editor, William B. Dickinson, Jr.

Contents

FOREWORD

ECONOMICS has been called the dismal science, but that description scarcely fits the bizarre situation facing the U.S. economy in mid-1970. What could be more intriguing than trying to make sense out of an economy which is about to produce $1 trillion in goods and services annually and, at the same time, may well be entering a severe recession? This paradox has all the drama and suspense of a good mystery novel, complete with potential villains.

What dastardly role, for example, has been played by the mysterious "They" on Wall Street—the institutional and mutual fund gunslingers who buy and sell as if on signal, making prices swing wildly and upsetting the nation's financial equilibrium? Or what of the little known members of the Federal Reserve Board secreted in their marble palace on Constitution Ave., who in manipulating the money supply drive up interest rates and demoralize the housing industry?

If America's affluent economy falls off the table in 1970 after 10 years of uninterrupted prosperity, the search for scapegoats will seek out these forces and many others, too. We have made the mistake of believing that, with only a little fine tuning, the economy could be kept on a relatively even keel despite uncontrolled government and personal spending. We could have both guns and butter, said President Johnson. The Congress and the people bought the illusion.

All evidence as this book goes to press is that economic cycles have not been repealed. The nation will have to pay the piper for inflationary excesses that could have been foreseen—and stopped—if common sense had prevailed. The reality is that a national economy, like a person, eventually must match its bills with hard dollars, not mere promises to pay. There is no such thing as a free lunch, even at the U.S. Treasury.

Our hope now is that the lesson will not be too expensive for the economy as a whole. Individuals and families already are feeling the pain of unemployment and rising prices. When enough pain goes around, you've got a recession. America's heady trillion-dollar economy is in trouble, and it's time to go back to the textbooks for a look into causes.

William B. Dickinson, Jr.
Editor

July 1970
Washington, D.C.

TRILLION-DOLLAR ECONOMY: PROSPERITY UNDER STRAIN

by

Richard L. Worsnop

1 9 7 0
June 17

TRILLION-DOLLAR ECONOMY: PROSPERITY UNDER STRAIN

SOMETIME late in 1970 or early in 1971, the United States will become the first country in the world to boast a trillion-dollar economy; that is, the gross national product—the market value of goods and services produced in the country in terms of 1970 dollars—will reach $1 trillion at an annual rate.[1] It hardly needs saying that such an achievement is prodigious—in particular because it comes barely more than a decade since G.N.P. first reached the $500-billion level. And that is not all: *Impact*, a weekly business and tax report, predicted on Dec. 22, 1969, that it would not be long before G.N.P. doubled again: "After taking nearly 200 years to log in its first trillion dollars, the U.S. economy will need only 10 more—the seventies—to achieve its second."

Still, the near-miracle of a trillion-dollar economy probably will receive mixed notices. It will be pointed out that around $250 billion of the $1 trillion G.N.P. represents post-1958 inflation. And numerous observers already have noted that gross national product makes no qualitative distinctions among its components—"The 25 cents spent on pretzels chewed listlessly in a cinema by some overweight matron enters the grand computation on the same terms as 25 cents spent on a bowl of soup by an emaciated pauper."[2]

Americans in general are more prosperous in 1970 than they were in 1960, despite the inflation that has occurred in the intervening period. Paradoxically, though, they appear to feel less sure of themselves and hence less well off materially. A staff correspondent reported from Miami in the May 18, 1970, issue of *U.S. News & World Report:* "Most people are making more and enjoying it less because, very often, they have less to enjoy." Sterling E. Soderlind, writing in the *Wall Street Journal,* July 7, 1969, asserted that rising discontent amid continuing prosperity "grows out of our accelerating aspirations."

---

[1] President Nixon, in a news conference of May 10, 1970, said: "I believe that by the end of the year we will have passed the trillion-dollar mark in terms of G.N.P."

[2] Edward J. Mishan, "The Spillover Enemy," *Encounter,* December 1969, p. 11.

He explained: "There is increasing evidence that our ascending affluence as we head into a trillion-dollar economy cannot match the expansion of our national goals. Tax-burdened citizens are aware that they no longer (if they ever did) live in an America - Is - Rich - Enough - To - Do - Anything - It - Wants - To - Do period."

Federal officials charged with formulating and carrying out economic policy likewise are frustrated as they attempt to cope with inflation, unemployment, and other pressing problems. If government spending were increased with a view to checking unemployment, the prospective federal budget deficit would increase also, thus further eroding the confidence of investors. If the Federal Reserve Board substantially expanded the supply of credit, inflation would become even more difficult to control than it is now. And compulsory or voluntary wage-price controls [3] have been rejected to date by President Nixon as inherently unworkable and unfair. A trillion-dollar economy, in short, is not easy to manage. As G. L. Bach, a Stanford University professor, told a recent bankers' symposium: "The dynamics of the economy are more complex than most of us had ever dreamed. The system is full of interactions and feedbacks, all operating with different time lags." [4]

The performance of the stock market over the past 18 months reflects investor confusion as to the true state of the economy. From a high of 985.21 on Dec. 3, 1968, the Dow Jones average of 30 industrial stocks slumped to 631.16 on May 26, 1970. The Dow average has since rebounded past the 700 level. The paper losses of stockholders in general since December 1968 are estimated at around $300 billion.

Current Strains and Imbalances in the Economy

The approach to a trillion-dollar economy comes at an awkward time—a time when "the nation seems stuck with both inflation and slump." [5] Inflation has been steep in terms of both consumer and wholesale prices. At the end of April 1970, the U.S. Bureau of Labor Statistics consumer price index stood at 134.0—in other words, 34 per cent higher than the average index for 1957-59. The wholesale price index, computed from the same base period, was 116.6 at the end of April. From March through May, consumer prices rose at an annual rate of 7.2 per cent, the highest annual rate since 1951. Food prices today

---

3 See "Anti-Inflation Policies in America and Britain," *E.R.R.*, 1965 Vol. II, p. 919.

4 Quoted in *Fortune*, May 1970, p. 153.

5 Gilbert Burck, "Hard Going for the Game Plan," *Fortune*, May 1970, p. 152.

are 30 per cent higher than a decade ago, and hospital costs are almost three times greater.

At the same time, signs of an economic slowdown are everywhere to be seen. Gross national product as measured in constant (i.e., 1958) dollars has declined for two consecutive quarters; two successive drops in "real" G.N.P. traditionally herald the onset of a recession. Unemployment, at 5.0 per cent, is now at its highest level since 1965.[6] Corporate profits are down by about 10 per cent from a year ago. The country's factories are operating at less than 80 per cent of capacity. High mortgage rates and the scarcity of credit caused new housing starts to drop by more than one-third in the last half of 1969; the consequent decline in vacancy rates has made rents soar in many areas.[7] And 1970 automobile sales are running more than one million units behind those of last year on an annual basis. The directors of a University of Michigan consumer survey said June 9 that "According to current indications, the 1970 recession will be the longest postwar recession" and that "A turning point cannot be expected earlier than at the end of the year 1970."

Nixon administration officials nevertheless contend that the economy is basically sound. For one thing, they note that personal consumption, business investment, and total federal, state and local government expenditures are continuing to rise. And they argue that while federal budget deficits are forecast for both fiscal 1970 and fiscal 1971, government spending will not rise sufficiently to add to inflationary pressure. President Nixon and his key economic advisers insist that their "game plan" for combating inflation is proceeding more or less on schedule and that results should be visible by the end of the summer.

The administration's game plan was devised chiefly by Arthur F. Burns, chairman of the Federal Reserve Board, and Paul W. McCracken, chairman of the President's Council of Economic Advisers.[8] Its aim is to create conditions under which natural economic forces will bring about disinflation. As originally conceived, the plan called for use of monetary and

---

[6] Seattle's unemployment rate of 8.1 per cent is the highest of any large U.S. city and was caused in large part by Boeing's layoff of 31,000 workers.

[7] See "Private Housing Squeeze," *E.R.R.*, 1969 Vol. II, p. 511.

[8] McCracken is reported to have been the one who "first appropriated the term Game Plan from football, a sport he greatly enjoys." The term has been called apt because "A game plan is not a book of rules or a detailed guide, but a strategy that seems most logical in the light of all available but necessarily incomplete information about the forces in the contest."—Gilbert Burck, *op. cit.*, p. 154.

fiscal policy to slow or halt the economy's growth for a time. To this end, the Federal Reserve would tighten the money supply and the Treasury would strive for a budget surplus. Then, as the economy began to feel the pinch, sales would be harder to make and costs would increase; business would be unable to raise prices at will and would even be forced to reduce them. Profits would be squeezed and unemployment would rise. At this point, according to the plan, business would be forced to reduce costs and to resist labor's inflationary wage demands. "Once the *rate of price increases* began to fall, monetary and fiscal policy could be eased. And provided the economy was not allowed to expand too fast, the rate of price increases, following a new momentum, would continue to decline." [9]

The game plan has succeeded to the extent that sales have been sluggish, profits have fallen, short-term interest rates are down, and unemployment has increased. So far, though, no progress has been made in bringing down the rate of consumer price increases. But the First National City Bank of New York, in its June economic letter, stated that a decline in the price-increase rate "may not be far off."

MAIN COMPONENTS OF THE GROSS NATIONAL PRODUCT

How well the administration's game plan succeeds in meeting its objectives will determine to some extent how soon the gross national product reaches the trillion-dollar level. Measured at current-dollar value, G.N.P. was $865.7 billion in 1968, $932.1 billion in 1969, and $959.6 billion (at an annual rate) in the first quarter of 1970. If G.N.P. should grow as much in 1970 as it did in 1969, it would fall just short of $1 trillion—$998.5 billion—for the year as a whole.

Gross national product, as noted, is the total national output of goods and services valued at market prices. It can be viewed in terms of spending categories. These comprise purchases of goods and services by consumers and by the government, gross private domestic investment by business, and net exports of goods and services. The goods and services included in G.N.P. are largely those bought for final use (excluding illegal transactions) in the market economy. There are a number of G.N.P. components, however, which represent imputed values; the most important of these is the rental value of owner-occupied dwellings. In short, G.N.P. measures the output attributable

---

9 Gilbert Burck, *op. cit.*, p. 154.

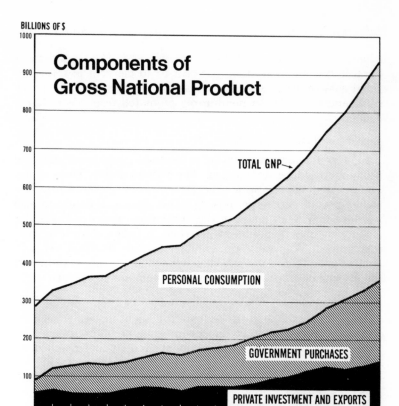

BILLIONS OF $

Components of Gross National Product

TOTAL GNP

PERSONAL CONSUMPTION

GOVERNMENT PURCHASES

PRIVATE INVESTMENT AND EXPORTS

1950 51 52 53 54 55 56 57 58 59 60 61 62 63 64 65 66 67 68 1969

to the factors of production—labor and property—supplied by residents of the United States.

The relative importance of the main components of G.N.P. has changed over the years. Between 1929 and 1969, the percentage of gross national product represented by business investment has remained relatively steady—around 15.7 per cent in 1929 as against 15 per cent in 1969. While personal consumption expenditures grew enormously in those four decades, they represented a declining proportion of total G.N.P. —around 75 percent in 1929 but only 61.6 per cent in 1969. On the other hand, government [10] purchases of goods and services have accounted for a steadily rising percentage of gross national product—8.2 per cent in 1929 vs. 23 per cent in 1969.

Milder but nonetheless significant shifts have occurred also in the relative importance of the three main categories of personal consumption expenditure—durable goods, [11] nondurable

---

[10] Including federal, state and local.
[11] Automobiles and automobile parts, furniture and household equipment, etc.

goods, [12] and services. [13] Between 1929 and 1969, spending on durable goods rose from 12 per cent to 16 per cent of total personal consumption, spending on services rose from 39 to 42 per cent, and spending on nondurable goods fell from 49 to 42 per cent.

EFFECTS OF INFLATION ON GROSS NATIONAL PRODUCT

In a sense, achievement of a trillion-dollar gross national product would be an illusion. The trillion-dollar figure represents current dollars which, because of inflation, are worth less than those of earlier periods. For this reason, economists also measure G.N.P. in terms of the purchasing power of the dollar of a given year or period rather than in terms of shifting current values. What is commonly referred to as "real" G.N.P. is stated in 1958 dollars. When viewed from this standpoint, the growth of gross national product seems less dramatic than it would otherwise.

The difference between the two approaches may be seen by comparing recent G.N.P. figures in terms of both current and 1958 dollars. As noted, gross national product had reached an annual rate of $959.6 billion in the first quarter of 1970—a seemingly substantial improvement over the 1969 full-year rate of $932.1 billion. "Real" G.N.P., however, actually declined from $727.5 billion in 1969 to an annual rate of $724.3 billion in the first quarter of this year.

By the same token, 1958 dollars were inflated in comparison with those of earlier periods, so G.N.P. totals before that year are even more widely at variance under the two approaches than are those since then. For example, gross national product in 1929, the last pre-depression year, aggregated $103.1 billion in current dollars but almost twice as much—$203.6 billion—in 1958 dollars. The distortion is greatest when the two criteria are applied to the years of the Great Depression. G.N.P. in 1933 was only $55.6 billion in terms of the deflated dollars of that year, but almost three times as great—$141.5 billion—in terms of 1958 dollars.

Neither approach to measuring G.N.P., in other words, is entirely satisfactory. The current-dollar yardstick tends to exaggerate declines in gross national product in times of depression and deflation, and to exaggerate increases in times of expansion and inflation. The constant-dollar standard tends to

---

[12] Food and beverages, clothing and shoes, gasoline and oil, etc.
[13] Housing, household operation, transportation, etc.

GROSS NATIONAL PRODUCT IN
CURRENT AND IN CONSTANT DOLLARS

(figures in billions)

Year	Current dollars	1958 dollars	Year	Current dollars	1958 dollars
1929	103.1	203.6	1950	284.8	355.3
1930	90.4	183.5	1951	328.4	383.4
1931	75.8	169.3	1952	345.5	395.1
1932	58.0	144.2	1953	364.6	412.8
1933	55.6	141.5	1954	364.8	407.0
1934	65.1	154.3	1955	398.0	438.0
1935	72.2	169.5	1956	419.2	446.1
1936	82.5	193.0	1957	441.1	452.5
1937	90.4	203.2	1958	447.3	447.3
1938	84.7	192.9	1959	483.7	475.9
1939	90.5	209.4	1960	503.7	487.7
1940	99.7	227.2	1961	520.1	497.2
1941	124.5	263.7	1962	560.3	529.8
1942	157.9	297.8	1963	590.5	551.0
1943	191.6	337.1	1964	632.4	581.1
1944	210.1	361.3	1965	684.9	617.8
1945	211.9	355.2	1966	749.9	658.1
1946	208.5	312.6	1967	793.5	674.6
1947	231.3	309.9	1968	865.7	707.6
1948	257.6	323.7	1969	932.1	727.5
1949	256.5	324.1	1970*	959.6	724.3

*Annual rate for first quarter.

---

understate the actuality in both cases, especially when the base year is rather distant in time from the one being measured. But since economics falls short of being an exact science, both approaches will continue to be used in the interest of arriving at a rough approximation of the truth.

CRITICISM OF EMPHASIS ON QUANTITY, NOT QUALITY

Conventional wisdom holds that economic growth—of which G.N.P. is the best-known indicator—is inherently good. An expanding economy provides more jobs, more goods, a better life for all. Lately, however, numerous authorities have begun to question these assumptions. Rising economic growth is now often equated with increasing damage to the environment. Even the concept of gross national product has come under scrutiny. G.N.P., it is pointed out, measures only quantity, not quality. It is asserted that a more sophisticated way of sizing up the economy is needed; a way that would take account of the drawbacks as well as the benefits of economic growth and reflect the difference between the two. Then, perhaps, policies could be shaped that would provide the optimum amount of growth and the least amount of contamination.

"When the United States was sparsely populated, emphasis on growth made good sense," a former member of the U.S. Forest Service recently wrote in *Science*. "Growth of many kinds permitted exploitation of the rich environment at an accelerating rate and provided a phenomenal increase in wealth."

> Growth still increases material wealth but has a growing number of unfortunate side effects, as each of us tries to increase his own benefits within an increasingly crowded environment. These spill-over effects, which were of minor importance when settlement was sparse and neighbors farther apart, are now of major consequence. For example, a firm may make the most money from a downtown tract of land by erecting a tall office building there. Construction of the building will add to the gross national product, and the builders will be hailed for their contribution to "progress." However, the building will add to traffic congestion, exhaust fumes, competition for parking, the need for new freeways, and social disorder. These problems, which must be handled by someone else, become part of the "environmental mess" or "urban crisis."[14]

Former Secretary of the Interior Stewart L. Udall, now an environmental consultant, spoke up for a "quality-of-life economy" in an address, June 9 in Chicago, before the First National Congress on Optimum Population and Environment. Anticipating opposition from economists, Udall said: "We are not...proposing a return to 'Walden Pond.' But we believe something is seriously wrong with a system that creates a fat life of empty affluence but can't even learn to recycle its wastes or build livable cities....The current economic system is based on an ideology of maximum production and maximum consumption. It may have been appropriate in 1932 or 1945, but it could lead us down a path to disaster in the remaining years of this century."

Economist Robert Lekachman makes the point that gross national product, far from discounting the deleterious effects of growth, adds them to its compendium of goods and services with "blind impartiality."

> If a new pulp mill discharges chemical wastes into a hitherto clean stream, the G.N.P. will go up, not only because of the mill's valuable output but also because other enterprises and municipalities located downstream from the polluter will be compelled to invest in cleaning devices required to return the water to usable condition. Similarly, the G.N.P. rises both with automobile sales

---

14 J. Alan Wagar, "Growth vs. the Quality of Life," *Science*, June 5, 1970, p. 1179.

and with the increased consumer expenditure for the cleaning of furniture, clothes, lungs, and bodies, necessitated by such purchases. [15]

It would of course be difficult to assign, say, a negative cost to such a "spillover effect" as aircraft noise and deduct it from that portion of gross national product represented by air transportation. Edward J. Mishan of the London School of Economics suggests that a more direct way of dealing with such problems would be to establish the principle of "amenity rights" in law. He asserts that "With respect to equity, it is a cardinal liberal tenet that every man should be allowed the freedom to pursue his own individual interest *provided* that in doing so he inflicts no harm on others." The primary effect of establishing amenity rights in law would be to make spillovers a part of the production costs of those responsible for them. Thus, an airline company would have the option of continuing all its services provided completely effective antinoise devices were installed or, to the extent they were not completely effective, of paying full compensation to persons suffering from the residual noise. [16]

Growth of Economy Since Colonial Times

TRANSFORMATION of the United States from a small, weak, predominantly agrarian society to an industrial colossus with an incipient trillion-dollar economy took place slowly, for the most part, and in spurts. The scarcity of reliable economic data from colonial times and the early years of the republic inhibits the search for explanations of how the change was accomplished. In general, though, it can be said that the country has been blessed with abundant land and mineral resources, a highly productive labor force, and a certain amount of plain luck.

At the end of the Revolutionary War, in 1783, the country was relatively prosperous but greatly dependent on foreign trade. Its chief commercial crops had to be sold abroad, and most manufactured products had to be imported. The new nation's economic assets included, among other things, an active commercial class, political institutions favorable to

15 Robert Lekachman, "The Poverty of Affluence," *Commentary*, March 1970, p. 40.
16 Edward J. Mishan, "The Spillover Enemy," *Encounter*, December 1969, pp. 8-9.

business enterprise, ample resources for manufacturing in the population centers of the Eastern Seaboard, and additional resources in the interior awaiting discovery and exploitation.

Although the United States is not inordinately endowed with the full range of important natural resources, it does possess in abundance some of the most important industrial minerals. North America, with only 14 per cent of the world's total land area, contains around one-fourth of global iron ore reserves. And the World Power Conference estimated in 1948 that it had close to one-half of the proven and probable coal reserves. The two minerals, of course, form the backbone of the steel industry.

Economic expansion was stimulated in the 19th century by expansion of both land and population. The original 13 colonies clustered along the Eastern Seaboard grew to a transcontinental country within 75 years of independence. In the first half of the 19th century, population doubled every generation. In more recent times, an intangible resource, education, probably has ranked in importance with coal, steel, and fertile farmland. It is estimated that the rising average educational level of the American work force in the past three decades alone has been responsible for perhaps two-fifths of increased labor productivity. [17]

Reliable and fairly complete data on the American economy did not begin to be compiled until around 1840. However, national income estimates all the way back to 1799 were made in 1939 by Robert F. Martin of the National Industrial Conference Board. In general, Martin's figures show a steadily rising national income for the United States between 1799 and 1859, but a sharp decline in per capita income between 1799 and 1829. From that time, income per head began to rise again, reaching by 1859 a figure ($292) substantially above that for 1799 ($210). Some economists believe that Martin underestimated per capita income from 1800 to 1840; but most scholars agree that economic development was slower in the first third of the 19th century than in subsequent years.

RISE OF INDUSTRY AND PROSPERITY AFTER CIVIL WAR

The relatively slow rate of economic growth in the period before 1840 can be attributed to the fact that agriculture was the largest single economic activity. Total farm production increased little faster than population. Industry, which provides

---

[17] John M. Peterson and Ralph Gray, *Economic Development of the United States* (1969), p. 12.

the greatest advances in income and living standards, was just beginning to experience an upsurge which, according to some authorities, took the United States to second position among the industrialized nations of the world by 1860. [18] It has been estimated that between 1799 and 1860 the portion of national income attributable to manufacturing rose from 4.8 per cent to 12.1 per cent. In the last two decades of that period, the 1840s and 1850s, economic growth was stimulated by extensive railroad construction as well as manufacturing expansion.

Although the Civil War destroyed much of the South's property, it proved a boon to industrial development in the North. Industry was not created by the war, but wartime demands greatly stimulated the industrial development which had been under way. As a result, "The years between the end of the Civil War and American entrance into World War I witnessed one of the most remarkable periods of the nation's economic growth." [19] In the years between 1867 and 1882, railroad construction was resumed and proceeded at a lively pace and the steel industry was developed. Another spurt of economic growth occurred around the turn of the century, when the electric utility and street-railway companies were built up.

It has been estimated that real gross national product doubled between 1869 and 1879. The U.S. Department of Commerce lists five-year averages dating from 1869 through 1921. Measured in terms of 1929 dollars, G.N.P. increased from a $9.1 billion average in the 1869-1873 period to $26.1 billion in 1889-1893 to $62.5 billion in 1912-1916—the last five-year period before American entry into World War I. Much of the post-Civil War increase in gross national product was attributable to expansion of manufacturing.

OLD BOOM-BUST CYCLES AND DEPRESSION OF 1930s

The course of the American economy over nearly two centuries of independence has been generally upward, but not in a straight line. Depressions, recessions and money panics of varying severity have been about as numerous as boom periods, though usually of shorter duration. Every major war, for example, has been followed sooner or later by an economic slump. The three decades after the Civil War were, as a whole, a period of striking growth in which the United States became the world's foremost industrial power. But each of

---

18 Britain was the leading industrial nation at that time.

19 Gilbert C. Fite and Jim E. Reese, *An Economic History of the United States* (1965), p. 296.

the three decades had its major depression—1873-1878 (the second longest on record), 1882-1885, and 1892-1894. And each of the three depressions was accompanied by a money panic— those of 1873, 1884, and 1893.

No previous depression could compare in length or severity, however, with the one heralded by the stock market crash of October 1929. [20] The blow fell with particular force at the end of seven years of prosperity during which real gross national product had increased by one-half. But from August 1929 to the low point of the cycle in March 1933, the economy established new records for contraction. Real net national product, [21] wholesale prices, and the money supply all declined by more than one-third. Unemployment rose from 3.2 per cent to 25 per cent of the labor force. The economy was, in effect, set back by more than a decade—in 1933, real gross national product was about 2 per cent under what it had been in 1922. By June 1932, the Dow Jones average of industrial stocks had toppled from its 1929 peak of 381 to 41.

This economic disaster, which was to last a decade, touched off a debate on whether a mature industrial economy such as that of the United States was fated to stagnate. Three conditions noted at the time seemed to indicate that stagnation was at least probable. First, population growth, both through immigration and natural increase, had markedly slowed; in the 1930s as a whole, population rose by only 7 per cent. Second, depletion of once-abundant natural resources was becoming apparent; by 1940, the United States was a net importer of timber and minerals. Finally, the well of technological innovation seemed to have run dry. In previous periods, such inventions and industries as the cotton gin, farm implements, railroads, electric power, and automobiles had provided a basis for general economic expansion. In the midst of the Great Depression, no new industries appeared to be providing stimulus for future growth.

Unparalleled Economic Expansion of the 1960s

Thoughts of stagnation were put aside during World War II, a period of great if artificial expansion. Between 1940 and 1945, gross national product more than doubled in terms of current dollars—from $99.7 billion to $211.9 billion. Moreover, the reconversion slump after the war lasted barely a year and was relatively mild.

---

[20] See "Wall Street: 40 Years After the Crash," *E.R.R.,* 1969 Vol II, p. 753.
[21] Gross national product minus the portion representing depreciation.

Recovery from a second postwar recession, in 1948-49, was well under way when the Korean War triggered a new boom in which gross national product increased by almost $80 billion from $284.8 billion in 1950 to $364.6 billion in 1953. The end of the war in June 1953 was followed within two months by the first of the three recessions that took place during the Eisenhower administration. The other two occurred in 1957-58 and 1960-61. Over-all economic growth slowed as the tempo of expansion-recession quickened in the 1950s. From 1947 to 1953, growth averaged 4.6 per cent a year; from 1953 to 1958, in contrast, the annual rate of growth slumped to an average of 1.3 per cent.

The recession inherited by President Kennedy "bottomed out" one month after he took office in January 1961, and economic expansion proceeded steadily through the remainder not only of his administration but also of the decade. Whether measured in terms of current or of 1958 dollars, the growth of gross national product in the 1960s was enormous. From 1960 to 1969, G.N.P. rose from $503.7 billion to $932.1 billion in current dollars and from $487.7 billion to $727.5 billion in terms of 1958 dollars.

The 1960s boom was made possible in part by the presence of elements that had seemed lacking in the economy in the 1930s. Technological change, increasingly related to scientific research, transformed existing industries and helped to establish such new ones as computers, self-developing film, and space communications, to name only a few. The development of the transistor facilitated the sale of television sets, radios, portable tape recorders, and other products. Articles once made of wood, steel, or plant and animal fibers increasingly were made of plastics, fiberglass, and artificial fibers.

Much recent and current technological innovation is the product of private or government-sponsored research and development or R & D. [22] It is estimated that R & D expenditures amounted to less than 1 per cent of gross national product in the 1920s but to more than 2 per cent in the 1960s. They may reach 3 per cent in 1970. R & D expenditures may be regarded as a form of investment—a use of resources currently to expand future production capabilities. During the 1950s, a close correlation was observed between the percentage of sales devoted to research in various industries and the rates of return on net worth in subsequent years.

---

[22] See "Government Research and Development,"*E.R.R.*, 1962 Vol. I, p. 41.

Increasing Complexity of Economic Policy

THE EXPANSION of the economy that began in 1961 was due in no small measure to federal government policies designed to produce orderly growth. The government's extensive spending and regulatory powers give it a commanding position in all sections of the economy. These powers, however, are of relatively recent origin. Most of the great regulatory agencies are less than 50 years old, and federal spending in peacetime was relatively small until after World War II. For most of the nation's history, the government lacked both the power and the inclination to influence economic trends in any substantial way.

INFLUENCE OF GOVERNMENT ON ECONOMIC ACTIVITY

The Civil War forced the federal government to assume for the first time a large—though short-lived—role in the economy. At the start of the war, tariff duties provided almost the only source of federal revenue, and a continuous budget deficit had been experienced since the recession of 1857. From $35 million in 1861, military expenditures alone jumped to $431 million in 1862 and by the end of the war reached $1 billion. To cover these staggering costs, the federal government raised tariffs, introduced a tax on personal income, and issued "greenbacks"—noninterest-bearing Treasury notes not redeemable in specie.

After the Civil War, Republican party leaders were anxious to return to "sound finance." It was regarded as prudent and moral to pay off the debt, reduce taxes, and restore the former value of the dollar in exchange for gold. Most taxes were rapidly cut or eliminated, [23] but federal receipts fell somewhat less rapidly because expanding production and imports yielded more revenue than expected. The Treasury used the resulting surplus to pay off debts and reduce the supply of paper money. This was, in effect, a tight-money policy, and prices fell steadily from the end of the war to the turn of the century.

The combination of restrictive monetary policy and expanding production in the years 1865-1900 led to recurrent money panics. These would occur when small banks all tried at once to

---

[23] The income tax was reduced in 1867 and eliminated in 1872.

withdraw reserves deposited in city banks, particularly those of New York City. Finally, after the Panic of 1907, widespread demand for banking reform arose. The Aldrich-Vreeland Act of 1908 provided temporary relief, a national Monetary Commission was appointed, and, in 1913, the Federal Reserve Act was signed.

The Federal Reserve Act did not create a strong central bank, as in many European countries, but it gave the government power to control the availability of money and credit. Of the tools used by the Federal Reserve to influence the level of economic activity, the discount rate is perhaps the best known. If the discount rate is raised, interest rates—particularly those on short-term loans—usually rise and credit tightens. Conversely, a cut in the discount rate ordinarily is followed by easier conditions in the money and capital markets. What an increase in the discount rate does is to put a brake on borrowing from the Reserve by member banks, and as the member banks pass along the higher rate to their customers, there is a brake on borrowing all along the line.

The monetary tool with the most immediate and widespread impact is the Federal Reserve Board's power to vary member reserve requirements. A change in reserve requirements alters the ratio of cash reserves that member banks must keep in relation to their deposits. Lowering the reserve requirements has the effect of making more of a bank's money available for lending, and raising it has the reverse effect. [24]

FAR-REACHING EFFECTS OF FEDERAL FISCAL POLICY

The government's monetary powers are matched by its fiscal powers. Fiscal policy, which sometimes runs counter to monetary policy, has to do with the exercise of federal powers to tax and spend. When tax revenues exceed federal expenditures, money is drawn out of the economy, thus producing a deflationary effect. Conversely, when expenditures exceed tax receipts, the additional money injected into the economy creates inflationary pressure.

Monetary policy is much more easy to manipulate than fiscal policy. The Federal Reserve System is largely insulated from outside pressure, and it may act to increase or decrease the money supply without the approval of Congress or the White House. The federal budget, on the other hand, is a political instrument subject to constant pulling and haul-

---

24 See "Money Supply in Inflation," *E.R.R.*, 1969 Vol. I, p. 143.

ing from the President, Congress, and private-interest groups. But federal spending is so great—more than $200 billion a year at present under the new "unified budget" concept [25] —that even small percentage shifts in spending have wide impact.

The current plight of the defense and aerospace industries illustrates the extent to which many sectors of the private economy have become dependent on the government. Cutbacks in government orders for military equipment have caused financial problems and extensive layoffs of workers at such giant companies as Boeing and Lockheed. North American Rockwell, prime contractor in the Apollo moon-landing program, was so badly pinched by contraction of federal spending on space that the price of its common stock slumped badly. But on June 5, 1970, the Air Force announced that North American Rockwell had been selected to build the airframe of a prototype bomber designed as a possible successor to the B-52. At the end of the first full day of trading following the announcement, the price of the company's shares on the New York Stock Exchange had risen by $2.50.

ACCEPTANCE OF KEYNESIAN THEORIES UNDER KENNEDY

In the years since World War II, the President's Council of Economic Advisers has played a leading role in setting the tone of economic policy. Established by the Employment Act of 1946, the council consists of three members appointed by the President with the advice and consent of the Senate. Its duties are to analyze the national economy and its various segments; to advise the President on economic developments; to appraise the economic programs and policies of the federal government; to recommend to the President policies for economic growth and stability; and to assist in the preparation of the economic reports of the President to Congress.

The council's influence on economic policy was especially pronounced in the 1960s, under the chairmanship of Walter W. Heller. Heller's ideas about national economic policy were essentially those of the Committee on Economic Development, which in turn were based on the writings of the British economist John Maynard Keynes. The C.E.D. program, first enunciated in 1947, urged that (1) "taxes be related to expenditures in terms of high employment, and that high employment be defined as 4 per cent unemployment"; (2)

---

[25] The most recent Budget Bureau estimate of fiscal 1970 federal spending was $205.6 billion. See "Federal Budget Making," *E.R.R.*, 1969 Vol. I, p. 1.

"budget deficits be accepted as a natural and useful stimulant in recessions"; (3) "budget surpluses are called for when the economy overheats"; (4) "periodic tax cuts might be needed to skim off the excessive tax burdens generated by economic growth."

Under Heller's leadership, the council stressed the then-novel concept of the "G.N.P. gap." The economy in 1961 had an unemployment rate of 6.7 per cent, and only 78.5 per cent of manufacturing capacity was in use. If unemployment were brought down to 4 per cent, it was calculated that gross national product could be increased by $40 billion a year. It followed that the way to bring unemployment down to 4 per cent was to create $40 billion of additional demand to fill this "G.N.P. gap."

A second new concept, related to the first, was that of the "full employment budget surplus." The original argument was that the federal budget deficit in 1961 was going to be around $3.5 billion. But if unemployment had been at the 4 per cent level defined as full, at least $8 billion in additional income-tax revenue would have been collected by the federal government. Thus, Heller argued, it was fair to say that the administration was aiming at what would have been a budget surplus if the country had full employment.

As implemented by Presidents Kennedy and Johnson, the policies recommended by the council proved highly successful. In the nearly three years of the Kennedy administration, gross national product increased by about $100 billion in current dollars, a rise of close to 20 per cent. In terms of 1958 dollars, the increase came to 5.5 per cent a year to early 1964. Despite this substantial increase in production, prices remained stable. Wholesale prices actually declined, and the cost of living rose by little more than 1 per cent a year. "For the first time since Grover Cleveland's day, a Democratic President had succeeded in stabilizing the internal value of the dollar." [26]

Inflation caused by expansion of the Viet Nam war in the mid-1960s undercut many of the economic gains set in motion during the early part of the decade. But the ideas advanced by Heller and his associates have become, as Norman Macrae of *The Economist* (London) pointed out last year, a part of "the conventional wisdom of American government." Macrae

---

[26] Seymour E. Harris, *Economics of the Kennedy Years* (1964), p. 7.

added that "The great achievements of the 1960s are that [the] governmental mechanism [for regulating the economy] has been reformed, and that the country has been set on a course of what many optimists now consider to be semi-automated economic expansion." [27]

DEBATE ON IMPOSITION OF WAGE AND PRICE CONTROLS

An important but unpopular economic policy of the Kennedy and early Johnson years called for voluntary adherence to wage-price "guideposts." The guideposts were first enunciated in the 1962 Economic Report of the President and were designed as an anti-inflationary tool. [28]

Today, with inflation rampant, President Nixon has been under some pressure to reinstitute voluntary wage-price controls such as the guideposts or even to ask Congress for compulsory controls such as were imposed during the Korean War. The President on many occasions has expressed strong opposition to economic controls, and he has been supported in that stand by, among others, Treasury Secretary David M. Kennedy. At a news conference in New York, June 10, 1970, Kennedy called wage and price controls a measure of "desperation" that would be resorted to only in a "very serious wartime economy."

Federal Reserve Board Chairman Arthur F. Burns, on the other hand, told a bankers' meeting at Hot Springs, Va., May 18, 1970, that "There may be a useful, albeit very modest, role for an incomes policy to play in shortening the period between suppression of excess demand and restoration of price stability." The term "incomes policy" refers to one form or another of voluntary wage and price restraints. Somewhat surprisingly, a Gallup Poll made public June 10 showed that 48 per cent of the persons questioned favored freezing wages and prices at present levels until the end of the war in Viet Nam; 41 per cent opposed such action, and 11 per cent were undecided.

Even if inflation were soon checked and the Viet Nam war ended without serious disruption of the economy, many serious problems would remain. The mounting debate on the quality of the environment eventually will become a debate on economic policy. The central question involved is whether unlimited growth may not be fatal in terms of its damaging spillover effects.

---

27 Norman Macrae, "The Neurotic Trillionaire" (special supplement to *The Economist*), May 10, 1969, pp. 25, 32.
28 See "Economic Controls," *E.R.R.*, 1969 Vol. II, pp. 610-613.

ADVERTISING IN A CONSUMER SOCIETY

by

Helen B. Shaffer

1 9 6 9
May 21

ADVERTISING IN A CONSUMER SOCIETY

THE CONTROVERSY over cigarette advertising, now headed for a showdown in Congress, points to a lack of consensus on how advertising in general should function in what is now being called a consumer society. That advertising is a central feature of such a society is a foregone conclusion. Few would seek its abolition, for advertising is so tightly locked into the country's complex marketing systems and so deeply implanted in the expectations of the people that it could not be dislodged without devastating effect on the economy, to say nothing of the national psyche. But though most Americans are comfortably attuned to the ubiquitous presence of advertising in their daily lives, they tend to be cynical about its operations.

The advertising industry therefore is in a curious public relations situation. Throughout the years of its great growth, advertising has come under continuing attack—by economists, social critics, moralists, government officials, consumer organizations. Many books, articles and plays have berated or ridiculed advertising or the advertising man and gained wide popular favor in so doing. Terms of derision, such as "the hucksters," have become a part of the language. Jokes about "Madison Avenue" and diatribes against advertising's materialistic influence on the American soul have grown commonplace. The oddity is that an industry which has thrived because of its skill in winning favor for its clientele should have had so much trouble creating a favorable image for itself.

LACK OF CLEAR POLICY ON ADVERTISING CONTROLS

Ambivalence of the public toward advertising has its counterpart in the vagueness of public policy on advertising controls. The validity of government regulation to prevent outright fraud is universally accepted. But three decades after federal regulatory powers over advertising were firmly established by law, a key question remains unanswered: how free should advertising be in a free-enterprise market? The question no longer pertains merely to questions of fraud or deceit, the ancient villains of anti-advertising crusaders. A more basic question has come to the fore: How free should advertising be to operate as a creator and conditioner of human wants, activities which affect both the economic well-being and the social temper of the nation?

This question became more insistent as the consumer economy expanded and as social problems associated with an affluent society multiplied. It is of particular pertinence at a time when the government is trying to cool down the economy. Indicative of the security of advertising's place in American life is the absence of any suggestion that advertising be curbed as an anti-inflationary measure.

The controversy over regulation of advertising approaches a new climax at a period when both consumer and advertiser are becoming increasingly sophisticated—the former less gullible, the latter more subtle or, to use the currently favored adjective of admen, more "creative" than in the past. Even those most offended by advertising's excesses might regret heavy-handed regulatory action that would stifle creative imagination in the hawking of goods and services, the point being that if there must be advertising, why not let it be clever and amusing? On the other hand, even friends of advertising have sometimes wondered at the ultimate consequences of unbridled efforts by master technicians of persuasion to promote human acquisitiveness.

CONTROVERSY OVER ADVERTISING OF CIGARETTES

How many additional television sets (or their future counterpart) will the prosperous American want, such questioners ask? Will the affluent society produce a satiety that will make the consumer indifferent to advertising's blandishments—perhaps to enjoy the clever commercial, but not to buy? What if more of advertising's creative genius were put to selling the values of a less avidly consuming society? These are some of the questions engaging the interest of the $18 billion advertising industry, its friends and its critics. Meanwhile, the most pressing immediate decision to be made—on cigarette advertising—is bound to influence future policy on the regulation of advertising. The basic question here is the degree to which the consumer needs to be protected from an innate susceptibility to the hawker's cry.

ADVERTISING: ESTIMATED EXPENDITURES
IN THE UNITED STATES
(in millions of dollars)

	1950	1955	1960	1965	1967
Total	$5,710	$9,194	$11,932	$15,255	$16,844
Newspapers	2,076	3,088	3,703	4,457	4,900
Radio	605	545	692	917	1,027
Television	171	1,025	1,590	2,515	2,923
Magazines	515	729	941	1,199	1,281
Direct mail	803	1,209	1,830	2,324	2,478
Outdoor	143	192	203	180	189

SOURCE: *Statistical Abstract of the United States 1968*, p. 783.

The central issue of advertising controls is more sharply defined in the case of cigarettes than in other cases in which the validity of advertised claims has been challenged. This is because of the gravity of the hazard to public health attributed to the advertised product (though still denied by the industry) and the great size of the industry which stands to suffer if critics of its advertising have their way.[1] Policies followed by the federal government reflect the dilemma it faces. On the one hand, it has thrown its influence, through its regulatory and health agencies, behind efforts to reduce cigarette consumption; at the same time, it has continued, through the Department of Agriculture, its traditional financial assistance to growers and marketers of tobacco.[2]

Two regulatory agencies have moved against cigarette advertising. The Federal Communications Commission proposed on Feb. 5, 1969, that cigarette advertising be barred altogether from radio and television. The Federal Trade Commission in a report on June 30, 1967, had voiced its belief that it was "imperative that adequate health warnings be included in all cigarette advertising." A 1965 law had provided that cigarette packages bear the warning that "Cigarette Smoking May Be Dangerous to Your Health"—a warning considered inadequate by F.T.C.—but the same law forbade any government agency to require inclusion of the warning in advertising of cigarettes.[3]

The latter prohibition is to expire on June 30, 1969. A bill to extend it is now before the House Commerce Committee,

---

[1] The U.S. tobacco crop returned $1.3 billion to growers last year. Cigarette sales totaled $8.9 billion. The tax return from the tobacco industry amounts annually to around $2 billion (federal), $2 billion (state), and $62 million (local).

[2] Government loans to support the price of tobacco totaled almost $130 million in 1968; losses on price-support loans amounted to $1.9 million. The government has been spending about $28 million a year on tobacco export subsidies and $240,000 to help finance advertising in foreign countries of cigarettes using American tobacco.

[3] See "Regulation of Cigarette Advertising," *E.R.R.*, 1967 Vol. II, pp. 866-867.

which on May 1 concluded 12 days of hearings on cigarette advertising and labeling bills. The hearings offered a forum for an exhaustive airing of irreconcilable positions. Unless a compromise measure can be devised, Congress may take no action at all. In that case, the F.T.C. will be free on July 1 to require inclusion of a health warning in all cigarette advertising. F.T.C. Chairman Paul Rand Dixon told the committee, April 22, that he was prepared to issue a regulation to that effect. If he does so, the industries affected will almost certainly attack the regulation in court as a violation of the free speech clause of the First Amendment to the Constitution.

F.T.C. already has taken action on cigarette ads under its authority to police advertising for deceptive and misleading material. The commission's regulations prohibit advertising of one brand of cigarettes as safer than another, and they require that tar and nicotine ratings cited in advertising be "factual, fair and not misleading."

The Federal Communications Commission had at its disposal a potentially more effective weapon against cigarette advertising on the air. This weapon was its authority to refuse to renew the licenses of broadcasting stations that failed to give balanced treatment to questions of public concern. On June 2, 1967, the commission ordered radio and TV stations that carried cigarette commercials to make available a significant amount of time for anti-smoking announcements.[4] The constitutionality of that rule, challenged by the broadcasting and tobacco industries as a restraint on free speech, was upheld on Nov. 28, 1968, by a 2-1 decision of the U. S. Circuit Court of Appeals for the District of Columbia. The case is now on appeal to the Supreme Court.

QUESTION OF FORBIDDING PROMOTION BUT NOT SALE

F.C.C.'s proposal to close the air waves to cigarette commercials raises not only the question of controlling *how* a product is advertised, but also the question of controlling *what* product is advertised. There is no precedent for a legal ban on advertising of a product in common use which may be freely sold in the consumer market. And though the justification advanced for such action is protection of the public from encouragement to use a potentially harmful product,

---

[4] Significant time has been interpreted to mean approximately one-third of the time devoted to cigarette commercials, and in comparable time-slots.

no action is proposed to restrict availability of the product in the consumer market or to forbid its advertising in other media.

Other consumer products have been barred at times from certain advertising media but not by government fiat. A ban on hard liquor commercials dates back to the pre-television era, when the liquor industry voluntarily agreed not to advertise over radio. The action was taken at a time when legislation to forbid liquor commercials was under consideration.[5] A number of mass circulation magazines—*Good Housekeeping*, for example—refuse advertisements of beer, wine or tobacco.

The National Association of Broadcasters' codes forbid a number of forms of advertising and the advertising of certain products. Suitability of the medium for advertising the product is often a guide. Thus, women's magazines accept advertisements for articles of personal hygiene which the broadcasting codes have barred from the air. Although violence by gunfire is a frequent ingredient of television programs, guns are rarely advertised on TV. The N.A.B. television code forbids advertising of the sale of firearms or ammunition by mail.

Cigarette (but not cigar, pipe or tobacco) commercials are forbidden in Great Britain, and the liquor industry there has voluntarily forsworn television advertising. Canada has banned broadcast advertising of liquor and of articles of feminine hygiene and has placed restrictions on the modes of advertising beer and wine. Proposals to ban cigarette advertising, pending in Parliament, have the support of the Canadian Medical Association, and the government itself conducts a vigorous anti-smoking campaign. The government-owned Canadian Broadcasting Corp. announced early in April 1969 that it would drop cigarette and other tobacco advertising when existing contracts expired.

EFFECT ON TELEVISION OF ANTI-SMOKING CAMPAIGN

In view of the portents, the industries involved may find it wise to forestall a U. S. government crackdown by voluntarily eliminating cigarettes from broadcast advertising.

---

[5] The rule was later incorporated into National Association of Broadcasters' codes which outlaw advertising of hard liquor on radio or television but permit wine, beer, and cocktail-mix commercials. The ban is not universally honored; at least one station, in New York City, carries liquor commercials.

Action to terminate cigarette advertising was announced in April by the Westinghouse Broadcasting Co., a nine-city chain of five TV and seven radio stations, and by two TV stations owned by the Washington Post-Newsweek Corp. The intention of RKO General to limit cigarette advertising on its radio and TV stations to brands of low tar and nicotine content, prematurely announced in mid-May, was reconsidered on the ground that such a policy decision had better be made on an industry-wide basis.

There are practical reasons why it would not be surprising if the broadcasting industry and cigarette manufacturers decided on their own to restrict or entirely abandon airing of cigarette commercials. A primary reason is distaste for further government interference in their methods of doing business. Litigation over an F.C.C. ban would keep the issue before the public and the outcome in doubt for a long time. Should the Supreme Court uphold the constitutionality of the ban, it would establish a most unwelcome precedent for all consumer goods industries, including advertising. The reaction in this quarter may be gauged by an advertising agency executive's comment on the F.C.C. proposal: "If the voice of legitimate business can be stifled in this manner," he said, "I wonder what product or services will be next obliterated by a statistical shadow. For any successful unopposed move inevitably will be repeated, expanded, extended." [6] National Association of Broadcasters President Vincent T. Wasilewski told the House Commerce Committee on April 21 that F.C.C.'s assertion of authority over cigarette advertising was "tantamount to a claim of power" to regulate advertising of all products.

Another reason for voluntary termination of cigarette advertising on the air is the apparent success of anti-smoking "commercials" produced for the American Cancer Society and other anti-smoking health agencies. How much they have contributed to a reported decline in cigarette consumption [7] cannot be measured exactly, but skillful projection of their message in brief spots (10 to 60 seconds) is recognized

---

[6] Ernest A. Jones, talk before Phoenix Advertising Club, March 10, reported in *Advertising Age*, March 17, 1969, p. 28.

[7] An Internal Revenue Service report on March 25 showed that "tax-paid removals" of cigarettes declined from 524.9 billion to 522.6 billion from fiscal 1967 to fiscal 1968. Other reports have indicated a decline of smoking in the civilian population, especially in younger smoking-prone age groups.

in the advertising profession.[8] "Promoters of anti-smoking messages have borrowed all the slickness of paid-for cigarette commercials—but with more hard sell," *Business Week* observed late last year.[9] The American Cancer Society has distributed anti-smoking films to every television station in the country, and a new voluntary organization, ASH (Action on Smoking and Health), has been monitoring stations and petitioning the F.C.C. to hold hearings on revocation or non-renewal of licenses of stations that fail to balance cigarette advertising with anti-smoking ads in comparable time-slots.[10] An estimated $50 million to $100 million worth of free broadcast time is now being made available for the anti-smoking crusade.

Less than a year ago, an advertising executive reported difficulty in inducing professional actors to appear in anti-smoking spots that he was filming for the American Cancer Society; the actors, he said, were afraid of losing lucrative opportunities to make cigarette commercials or to appear in shows sponsored by cigarette companies.[11] Since then the situation has changed. "The number of actors who are refusing to do cigarette commercials is growing every day," the head of a talent agency reported recently.[12] Actress Doris Day and orchestra leader Lawrence Welk stipulated in their latest contracts that no cigarette company might sponsor their TV shows. Actor Tony Curtis on March 11 became national chairman of the Cancer Society's I.Q. (I Quit Smoking) Program; he will appear in anti-smoking "commercials" and is expected to recruit other celebrities of the entertainment world.

Cigarette producers spend more than $200 million a year—three-fourths of their advertising dollar—on television advertising. More than 7 per cent of television's income comes from this source. Loss of the cigarette accounts might not be serious for the industry, however, because there is strong demand for the prime time now occupied by cigarette com-

[8] Perhaps the most effective of all was a one-minute spot filmed on July 17, 1968, featuring William Talman, known to TV audiences as the prosecutor in the Perry Mason series. Talman, who had been a heavy smoker, was in a late stage of lung cancer. He appealed to the TV audience to quit smoking or not take up the habit. Six weeks later he died of the disease.

[9] "Anti-Cigarette Commercials," *Business Week*, Dec. 21, 1968, p. 79.

[10] ASH was formed by John F. Banzhaf 3d, a young lawyer, who filed the complaint that resulted in the 1967 F.C.C. ruling. On March 23, 1969, Banzhaf announced formation of LASH (Legislative Action on Smoking and Health) to serve as "the legal action arm of the anti-smoking community." On Apr. 2 he filed petitions with F.C.C. accusing nine stations of laxity in observance of the balanced-program rule.

[11] Richard J. Lord, quoted in *New York Times*, July 3, 1968.

[12] *New York Times*, March 6, 1969.

mercials. How the disappearance of TV cigarette commercials would affect cigarette consumption is debatable. *Business Week* quoted an industry man who said: "I'd like to see us legislated off TV. Then the networks would not be compelled to run these anti-smoking spots and that would help a great deal." [13]

Unlike the producers of many other consumer products, the tobacco industry is hampered in any effort to enlarge the total domestic market for its product by public sentiment (and industry codes) against advertising aimed to induce young people to take up the smoking habit. Marketing of cigarettes has therefore become more competitive than ever, with advertising directed mainly toward an effort to capture for a particular company or brand a larger share of a more or less stable if not declining total market. Removal of all cigarette advertising from a single medium might well have a neutral effect on the present division of retail sales.

Certainly it would spur advertisers to new heights of competitive endeavor in other media. The billboard industry, for one, is standing by to catch the windfall. "With the F.C.C. threatening to close down TV for cigarette advertising, you can be sure we've had some meaningful talks with tobacco people," the president of an outdoor advertising (billboard) company told an advertising club meeting recently.[14]

Advertising's Long Struggle for Stature

OBJECTIONS to cigarette advertising long predate the current controversy, which was sparked by the finding of a probable relationship between cigarette smoking and lung cancer, reported in 1964 by the U. S. Surgeon General's Advisory Committee on Smoking and Health. The fact is that not only cigarette advertising but advertising in general has provoked criticism from the beginning. The criticism has been a source of distress to advertising men, whose sensitivity to complaints about their activities has often been noted. No matter how worn by frequent repetition, every

13 "Anti-Cigarette Commercials," *Business Week*, Dec. 21, 1968, p. 79.

14 *Advertising Age*, March 17, 1969, p. 55.

jibe has inevitably called forth a riposte from a member of the advertising fraternity. It has been the same in other countries where advertising of consumer goods is preeminent. A British professor of advertising has spoken of "a certain monotony" in the debate because "the same arguments recur" on both sides.[15]

The enormous success of an industry which in this country has grown 1½ times as fast as the Gross National Product since World War II would seem to indicate that advertising had little to fear from its critics. A recent scholarly study showed that the severe critics comprise only a small minority, and that Americans generally enjoy advertising and have "little disposition . . . to deny that advertising has a legitimate role in American life." Knocking ads was found to be "a convenient topic for ritualized griping"; much of the complaining was not intended to be taken very seriously. Most cheering of all for the industry was the conclusion that only 1 per cent of a population sample questioned in the mid-1960s thought more regulation of advertising was needed.[16]

Nevertheless, the industry has reason for concern. The persistent criticism, the crusading intensity of the critics, and their exposure of abuses that victimize the poor or unsophisticated nourish a movement which industry leaders refer to with disfavor as "consumerism." Advertisers often proclaim their devotion to the consumer, but "consumerism" is something else again. "Consumerism" aims to substitute for the arts of persuasion, which constitute the very heart of the advertising enterprise, plain information about the product to be sold. The most-feared consequence of "consumerism" is the imposition of more government controls.

EARLY WARNINGS OF DECEIT IN THE MARKETPLACE

Criticism of advertising is apparently rooted in the potential buyer's ingrained suspicion of the seller. "He who first objected to the babbling barker of the Babylonian tradesman was the unknowing progenitor of a long line of critics." [17] Plato referred to merchants who "do not know which food is good for us and which is bad but say that everything they sell is good." Cicero said: "For the dealer will gain nothing except by profuse lying, and nothing is more disgraceful than untruthful huckstering."

[15] Walter Taplin, *Advertising: A New Approach* (1963), pp. 3-5.

[16] Raymond A. Bauer and Stephen A. Greyser, *Advertising in America: The Consumer View* (1968), pp. 88-90.

[17] *Ibid.*, p. 4.

"The concept of the market as a place of deceit and the seller as a deceiver" [18] was firmly established when advertising began, in the 17th century, to develop as an important instrument of the selling function. Preposterous claims made for the plethora of nostrums and beautifiers that were hawked in their time justified the contempt expressed by many literary figures of the 17th-19th centuries. Daniel Defoe in *Journal of the Plague Year* expressed outrage over the exploitation of the ignorant in 1665 by hawkers of pills, potions and charms.

Despite its critics, advertising flourished when it found a natural medium in newspapers and magazines. In 1759 Samuel Johnson wrote in *The Idler:* "Advertisements are now so numerous that they are very negligently perused, and it is therefore become necessary to gain attention by magnificence of promise and by eloquence sometimes sublime and sometimes ridiculous. . . . I cannot but propose a moral question to these masters of the public ear, whether they do not sometimes play too wantonly with our passions."

It was the same in the American colonies. Benjamin Franklin, "father of American advertising," [19] was a vigorous salesman and composer of advertising copy. His ad for his Pennsylvania Fireplace (Franklin stove) took the familiar line of scare copy: He warned that women, who sit around the house a great deal, are subject to chills that could lead to "rheums and reflexions which fall into their jaws and gums," a condition which had "destroyed early many a fine set of teeth in these northern colonies."

INDUSTRY-LAUNCHED TRUTH-IN-ADVERTISING DRIVE

The relatively low opinion of advertising held by the educated classes in the 19th century was indicated by the fact that certain quality magazines refused it and others did not bother to solicit it. The custom was for the advertiser to make a personal visit to a publisher's office, request permission to place an announcement of his wares, and, if the ad was accepted, to pay in advance, a "requirement that reflected the general view that puffing was a shady pursuit." [20]

Periodicals could afford to be cavalier toward advertisers so long as the major part of their revenue came from sub-

---

[18] Dexter Masters, *The Intelligent Buyer and the Telltale Seller* (1966), p. 12.
[19] S. Watson Dunn, *Advertising: Its Role in Modern Marketing* (1961), p. 19.
[20] Frank Rowsome, Jr., *They Laughed When I Sat Down* (1959).

scribers. With the rapid development of national and regional marketing systems, advertising became increasingly important as a means both of selling consumer goods and of underwriting the costs of publishing. Furthermore, readers of mass circulation newspapers and magazines seemed to like the ads. James Gordon Bennett, publisher of the *New York Herald,* "was one of the first newspapermen to realize that people buy papers for the advertisements as well as the news items." [21]

As advertising grew and began to take its modern shape within the marketing structure,[22] it became increasingly concerned with its public image. The preposterous and often dangerous medicine ads were an obvious target for reform. An exposé of false claims of patent medicines, published in *The Ladies Home Journal,* sparked a clean-up movement that induced some publications to screen out objectionable advertising. Then the Associated Advertising Clubs of America (later Advertising Federation of America) sponsored a "truth-in-advertising" campaign that led to the formulation in 1911 of a voluntary code for ethical advertising. In the same year, *Printers' Ink,* advertising's trade journal, sponsored a model state law providing penalties for false and misleading advertising. Within a few years two-thirds of the states had adopted laws of this kind.

Advertising's image improved during World War I when the industry contributed its skills to the war effort. But advertising did not come fully into its own until the hectic, booming, get-rich-quick, spendthrift 1920s. "For the first time, marketing (including advertising and selling) was not only respectable—it was looked on as equal to production. The high-pressure salesman and the high-pressure advertising man were . . . the darlings of the 1920s. Both helped the growth of the mass markets needed to support our production facilities." [23]

Advertising grew more clever. It catered to the individual's desire to be young, beautiful, rich, admired. Consumers learned from advertising of such previously unrecognized menaces to their health, beauty and success as halitosis, pink

---

[21] Dunn, *op. cit.,* p. 24.

[22] The advertising agency came into the picture in the late 19th century, market surveys in the early 20th. One of the first surveys was door-to-door questioning of housewives preparatory to launching an advertising campaign for canned baked beans. ("The best way is to let us cook them for you," the ad said.)—Dunn, *op. cit.,* p. 27.

[23] Dunn, *op. cit.,* p. 31.

tooth brush, tattletale gray, and they simultaneously learned of the one product that would banish the threat to their happiness. What had been luxuries for the few became necessities for the many—an automobile, "moderne" furniture, liquid shampoo, a host of household appliances.

Critics raised their voices against advertising in the 1920s, but few paid much attention to them. "Aside from a few carping eggheads, criticism of admen and advertising was practically stilled in the 1920s as the nation wallowed in its first rousing prosperity." [24] The advertising man was admired as the go-getter who spurred the economy onward and upward. The American Economic Association hailed advertising as an "essential of present-day civilization without which further progress is inconceivable." President Coolidge, addressing the American Association of Advertising Agencies in 1926, said: "Advertising ministers to the spiritual side of trade. It is a great power which is inspiring and ennobling the commercial world. It is all part of the greater work of the regeneration and redemption of mankind."

PEAKING OF CRITICISM IN THE DEPRESSION DECADE

After the bubble broke in 1929, advertising fell to its lowest estate. The spendthrift consumer of the 1920s was now so lacking in purchasing power he could not even afford necessities. Advertising adapted to the change by stressing economy, price and durability, though there remained escapist ads to tempt those worn down with the troubles of the time. But the advertising man was no longer the popular figure he had been.

Criticism which had gone unheard in the boom decade found a large audience in the 1930s, when every facet of the economic system was undergoing re-examination in a search for causes of the disaster. Stuart Chase and Thorstein Veblen, who had denounced advertising during the 1920s as a source of economic waste, were now joined by a host of writers who found a responsive public. F. L. Schlink and Arthur Kallet in *100 Million Guinea Pigs* (1932), a depression era best-seller, lambasted advertising not only for specific instances of absurdity or deceit but also for its fundamental character, which to them resembled that of an unscrupulous exploiter of the consuming public. These views

---

[24] Joseph J. Seldin, *The Golden Fleece* (1963), p. 21.

were echoed by contributors to a 1934 issue of the influential *Annals* of the American Academy of Political and Social Science devoted to *The Ultimate Consumer: A Study in Economic Illiteracy.*

Modern "consumerism," which so disturbs the advertising industry today, gained impetus in this period. The movement was directed not only to correction of deceit or other faults of advertising, but also to dissemination of concrete information on consumer products that would undercut the fantasies of the advertisements. Consumers' Research, founded in the late 1920s to make comparative tests of the quality of competing goods in the consumer market, gained many subscribers during the depression, and a similar organization, Consumers' Union, was founded in 1936.

Another angle of the consumer movement was the introduction in schools of consumer guidance courses, which taught future householders how to spend their money wisely and incidentally to resist the blandishments or wiles of the advertiser. The movement's greatest achievement was consumer protection legislation. Congress in 1938 strengthened the authority of the Federal Trade Commission to take action against false or misleading advertising that victimized the consumer.[25]

World War II restored much of advertising's prestige. Not only did the industry, through the War Advertising Council, carry out many public service campaigns, the shortage of consumer goods put a curb on high-keyed consumer product advertising. Advertising naturally boomed again in the postwar period and so did the criticism. The postwar population offered consumer goods industries a market unprecedented for its size, rapidity of growth, buying power, and hunger for goods. Competition for the bonanza market was reflected in a spate of aggressive advertising which made increasing use of the new and most potent advertising medium of all for consumer goods—television.

But a new style of life was taking shape, epitomized by young suburbanites who were less responsive than preceding generations to familiar advertising gambits. Many in this new army of goods-hungry consumers had grown up in low-

---

[25] Previously, F.T.C.'s authority over advertising had extended only to "unfair trade practices" that harmed a business competitor. See "Advertising Controls," *E.R.R.*, 1956 Vol. II, pp. 811-826.

consuming households; hence they were fashioning their own rather than following the buying patterns and predilections of their parents. This, together with the plethora of competing goods (dozens of different cake mixes and soap powders) available to them on the same supermarket shelf contributed to a breakdown of "brand loyalty" which advertising campaigns of the past had so carefully built up.

MOTIVATION RESEARCH ON THE ELUSIVE CONSUMER

Uncertainty about the character of the postwar consumer market and the high cost of launching new or "improved" products, considered necessary in so competitive a market, caused advertisers to turn more than ever to market research. The rather simple surveys of the past, which had sent out doorbell ringers to ask housewives what they thought of canned beans or cold-storage chicken, would no longer do. The consumer goods industry, with its now indispensable adjunct, the advertising industry, turned to psychologists and social scientists for exhaustive studies of the consuming public. Motivation research, which sought to uncover the inner mainsprings of the consumer buying urge, entered the marketing picture.

> In an age of abundance, the motivation researchers argued, the noneconomic reasons why people bought were also mostly nonrational. . . . If pressed for reasons, the consumer would offer surface reasons which served to protect [his] . . . view of himself as a rational human being. Only skillful psychological probing could get at buying motivations that lay entombed in the subconscious.[26]

The value of motivational research has been the subject of much debate within the advertising profession. Some denounced it as pseudoscientific, faddish, or useless as a guide to developing effective advertising campaigns.

Studies of the hows and whys of consumer behavior, however, have continued unabated. Aside from studies undertaken preparatory to launching specific advertising campaigns, the consumer is a relatively popular subject for academic research. Ph.D. candidates in a number of universities are undertaking research in this field, some of them with grants from the American Association of Advertising Agencies Educational Foundation. Typical of subjects of current study are: How do consumers make decisions to buy? How can advertising help overcome the sense of risk a consumer feels when contemplating the purchase of an ex-

---

[26] Seldin, *op. cit.*, p. 236.

pensive item? What are the long-term effects of repeating the same ad, or how long should an ad run before changing it? Harvard's Graduate School of Business Administration recently published a book reporting on an intensive study of what the public thinks of advertising generally and of specific ads in particular.

The consumer remains the great unsolved mystery of advertising. "The Person Nobody Quite Understands" is the title of an article on the consumer in a business magazine. "An unpredictable cuss," the magazine's editor called him.[27]

Current Trends in Appeals to Consumer

ADVERTISING now is undergoing a so-called "creative revolution" brought on by a new breed of young writers, artists, designers, photographers, and idea men who are disdainful of hallowed precepts and past taboos. The creators of a new style of advertising went into business for themselves and were so successful in winning accounts [28] that the older and more staid agencies began to hire young ad-makers of the same sort, giving them plenty of scope and paying them higher salaries than some account executives.

Ads created by the new breed tend to be witty, novel, pithy, shocking, sexy, artistic, visually "way out," imaginative, understated, surrealist, or just plain nutty. "They have brought wit and dash and modern graphic design to advertising, which hitherto was undistinguished and boring as well," writes an admirer of the new-style admen.[29] And another rejoices that "Never has advertising been so honest, free and pleasantly outrageous." [30] The breakthrough ads that cleared the way for the new style were "Think Small" for Volkswagen and "We're Only No. 2" for Avis (car rental).

[27] "The Person Nobody Quite Understands," *Nation's Business*, May 1968, p. 48, and "What Consumers Won't Buy," *Nation's Business*, November 1968, p. 7.

[28] "Twenty to 30 new [creative] agencies that sprang up [in 1967] . . . took about $150 million in aggregate billings away from the older agencies."—"Ad Agencies Have New Campaign—Efficiency," *Business Week*, Apr. 20, 1968, p. 154.

[29] Charles Sopkin, "What a Tough Young Kid With *Fegataccio* Can Do on Madison Avenue," *New York Times Magazine*, Jan. 26, 1969, p. 34.

[30] Rodney Campbell, "Advertising at the Dawn of the Age of Aquarius," *Careers Today*, March 1969, p. 21.

The basic purpose of the new advertising is not different from that of the past: it is still, above all, to catch and hold the attention of the passerby, the casual reader, the unmindful watcher. In today's advertisement-saturated environment, it is becoming increasingly difficult to create an ad with impact. Research has shown that much of today's advertising effort is wasted. "In a study commissioned by the advertising business itself, it was found that 85 per cent of all advertising does not even get looked at." [31] In a medium suffused with overblown puffs and unbelievable promises, cleverness and candor have proved an effective pitch.

Another reason for the success of the newcomers is that, being young, they are in tune with young America. The consuming public is getting younger; more than half the population is under 28 and even older people are influenced by youth in their buying decisions as never before. The "creative revolution" adman, therefore, is following an old advertising principle: to convey the message in terms of the tastes, predilections, and susceptibilities of the potential buyer. And today's consumer is considered too knowing to be taken in by the simple hyperboles ("Ours is the best") or the threats of disaster ("Buy our product or—") of older advertising styles. "You're going to have to abandon all those past principles of advertising," a veteran marketing specialist warned recently. ". . . Young people seem to like it honest, loose, irreverent, and uncompromising." [32] General Motors President Edward N. Cole told the Sales Executives Club of New York on Sept. 10, 1968, that a "new breed of consumers . . . has become quite immune to the big sell" and that "only the most intelligent, direct and personal appeal can hope to gain consumers' attention."

CHANGES IN CONTEST WITH CONSUMER PROTECTORS

The "creative revolution" in advertising may provide an answer to those critics who have complained, as has F.T.C. Commissioner Paul Rand Dixon, of "the banality, the appeals to greed and to vanity that shout from every page of advertising." [33] But though the revolution is producing a number of brilliantly imaginative and artistically striking advertisements, especially those which the advertising in-

---

[31] "But Does It Sell?" *Britannica Book of the Year 1967*, p. 68.

[32] E. B. Weiss, "Is Creative Advertising a Young Business?" *Advertising Age*, Sept. 2, 1969, p. 41.

[33] Annual Government Affairs Conference of American Advertising Federation, Washington, D. C., Feb. 17-19, 1969.

dustry contributes to public service programs, it is far from complete. To a large extent, the old styles persist, as do the old criticisms.

The quarrel between the advertising industry and the consumer protection movement may be moving into a new phase. After years of mutual recrimination, there are indications that industry leaders are preparing to make their peace with the movement if only to keep it from getting further out of hand. Howard Bell, president of the American Advertising Federation, said last Sept. 12 that the A.A.F. was ready to work with all organizations active in consumer affairs. He reiterated the traditional industry position that protection of the consumer against the few scoundrels who prey on the unwary was all right, but that in the last analysis the businessman—producer and advertiser—is the best protector of consumer interests because of his stake in having a satisfied customer.

Arthur C. Fatt, advertising executive and member of the National Marketing Advisory Committee to the U. S. Department of Commerce, made the same point in a recent article attacking current proposals for more consumer protection legislation. But he called on business to join government in studying "whether a problem truly exists, what the extent of this problem is, and how effective the proposed action will be in accomplishing its avowed intent." [34]

E. B. Weiss, "considered by many people to be the country's foremost 'trend spotter' in marketing," according to the *Harvard Business Review*,[35] chided marketing leaders for piously denouncing consumer protection proposals instead of making plans "to guide present consumer legislation to beneficial socio-economic ends." Something of a gadfly in his field, Weiss, who has been a regular columnist in *Advertising Age* for a dozen years, has urged the advertising industry to take seriously the charges brought against it instead of responding with hackneyed paeans of self-praise. "These charges have never been objectively studied," he said, and they "will not be buried by fervent 'free enterprise' pleas, by slanted studies, or by angelic poses."

---

[34] "Let's Take the Politics Out of Consumerism," *Nation's Business*, January 1969, p. 86.
[35] Foreword to article by E. B. Weiss, "Marketers Fiddle While Consumers Burn," *Harvard Business Review*, July-August 1968, p. 45.

There are social critics who complain that perpetual hawking of new goods affects the national character unfavorably. An author of this persuasion recently complained that advertising "must foster acquisitiveness, envy, extravagance, ostentation, and, above all, vanity." Americans were said to be raised from childhood to function primarily as consumers rather than producers, as spenders rather than earners. "The consuming culture is directed at proliferating . . . needs so that men, women and children must buy and buy to escape feeling deprived. . . ." [36]

CONSUMER GOODS ADVERTISING AND SOCIAL UNREST

The conflict between the consuming society and the Puritan ethic of thrift and self-denial has been noted by both friends and critics of advertising. "For continued economic growth," a marketing professor has warned, ". . . this feeling of guilt [over our abundance] must be overcome."

> American consumers still adhere to many puritanical concepts of consumption, which are relevant in an era of scarcity but not in our economy of abundance. . . . [We] must change our consumption philosophy . . . bring it in line with the age of plenty. To do so the abundant life style must be accepted as a moral one. [37]

This view of the good life is hospitable to the fullest use of advertising to stimulate consumer wants. But a grimmer consequence of unbridled consumer goods advertising has come to the fore with the growth of crime, rioting, and social protest by the have-nots of the affluent society. An article in the current issue of the *Harvard Business Review* warned the business community that it should consider the effect of "the tantalizing television advertisements" on members of the "persistent proletariat" who seem unable to break out of the poverty trap. Looking to the future, the author wrote:

> [The] advertisements that are so widely presumed to grease the wheels of commerce will increasingly play the powerful revolutionary role of creating dissatisfaction and unrest among those whose appetites are whetted by the televised standard of living, but whose means never come within reach. The more effective the advertisements, the greater the discontent. [38]

The social effects of advertising in a consumer society obviously extend far beyond the mere selling of goods.

[36] Ronald Segal, *The Americans: A Conflict of Creed and Reality* (1969), pp. 58, 98, 138.

[37] William Lazer, "Marketing's Changing Relationships," *Journal of Marketing*, January 1969, pp. 4-6.

[38] Theodore Levitt, "The New Markets," *Harvard Business Review*, May-June 1969, p. 61.

WALL STREET: 40 YEARS AFTER THE CRASH

by

Hoyt Gimlin

1 9 6 9
Oct. 8

WALL STREET: 40 YEARS AFTER THE CRASH

FORTY YEARS have elapsed since Black Thursday, Oct. 24, 1929, the day the great stock market crash began. The memory of 1929 haunts millions of stock traders in the present year of declining market prices and other Wall Street problems. Although the confidence of investors recovered long ago from the disastrous events of 1929, the notion lingers that another such crash may not be altogether impossible. For Wall Street, so surfeited in prosperity for so long, the past year has had a chastening effect.

The year began with speculation by financial writers as to how soon the Dow-Jones industrial average, perhaps the best-known barometer of prices on the New York Stock Exchange, would reach the long-awaited 1,000 mark, a symbolic capstone to the bull market of 1967 and 1968. But, instead of rising, prices went down with only brief interruptions from the historic high of 985 in December 1968 to a 1969 low—thus far—of 801.96 on July 29.

The 18.6 per cent decline in the Dow average was the fourth biggest in the past 20 years,[1] and it lasted longer than the six-month average duration of eight previous major market slumps. Paper losses incurred by late summer were reckoned in some quarters to have reached $100 billion—losses shared by many of the estimated 26 million Americans who own stock directly and by 100 million others who do so indirectly, through pension funds and in other ways.

Some individual losses were greater than indicated by the "Dow," because it is an arithmetical average of 30 leading blue chip stocks, those of the nation's big industrial corporations.[2] Among the more volatile "glamour" and "performance" stocks, those which have attracted most attention

---

[1] Exceeded by declines in the bear markets of 1957 (19 per cent), 1961-62 (25), and 1966 (25).

[2] The Dow average may be less representative of the entire stock market than the Standard & Poor Average (of 500 stocks), but it is given wide currency by transmission over the Dow-Jones news ticker, the so-called "broad tape" which serves the financial community.

43

in recent years, individual issues showed losses of 50 per cent and more. "Conglomerates," new corporations formed by mergers of businesses in unrelated fields, tended to suffer heavily in the market decline.

A veteran stock broker described the scene this way: "There are the conservative investors, many of them retired people with plenty of money, who invested for long-term growth and a good income. They are sitting tight on quality stocks . . . and they aren't worried."

> There's a new type of aggressive investor who's done so well in recent years that he takes profits for granted. He counts on the stock market to pay for his new car or a trip to Europe. This fellow is all shook up. . . . Then there's the small gambler, out for a killing. Poor devil, he's been shot full of holes, but he's philosophical about it—for him it's been a sad trip to Vegas. Finally, there are a great many inexperienced investors who last year put their savings into stocks or mutual funds, because some wise guy told them this was a sure hedge against inflation. Some of them are stunned by what they've lost, at least on paper, and they are deeply disillusioned with the stock market.[3]

By common agreement, inflation has helped to produce dramatic increases in both volume and price on the stock market since 1966. The government's efforts to control inflation, conversely, are considered to have been one cause of the 1969 decline. Since December 1968, the Federal Reserve Board has pursued a tight-money policy intended to soak up excess lendable funds of commercial banks.[4] Money is the life-blood of securities markets; and it is especially needed to sustain a rising market.

Stock investors have been troubled this year also by fear that Congress would change capital-gains tax rules. Under present law, profits on sales of stock owned for more than six months are treated as long-term capital gains and taxed by the federal government at a maximum rate of 25 per cent. A tax reform bill passed by the House on Aug. 8, now pending in the Senate, would raise the rate to 32½ per cent and make that rate applicable only on gains from sales of stock held for at least one year. The House bill also would tighten tax rules on deduction of interest on money borrowed to finance securities purchases. These changes drew strong

---

[3] Quoted by Charles J. Rolo, "When Wall Street Catches the Flu, 26 Million Americans Ache," *New York Times Magazine*, Aug. 31, 1969, p. 12.

[4] See "Money Supply in Inflation," *E.R.R.*, 1969 Vol. I, pp. 145-162, and "Economic Controls," *E.R.R.*, 1969 Vol. II, pp. 598-599.

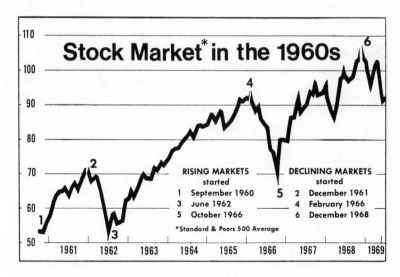

Stock Market* in the 1960s

RISING MARKETS started
1 September 1960
3 June 1962
5 October 1966

DECLINING MARKETS started
2 December 1961
4 February 1966
6 December 1968

*Standard & Poors 500 Average

opposition from Wall Street at hearings before the Senate Finance Committee.[5]

REDUCED BROKER PROFITS AND SEARCH FOR CAPITAL

When stock prices fall, trading tends to decline—unless there is panic selling. The stock market has remained "orderly" in 1969 despite extensive losses. The lack of panic selling has been attributed, first, to public confidence that prices will eventually rebound and, second, to the fact that stocks cannot now be bought on borrowed money to anything like the extent possible 40 years ago.

Brokerage houses have been doubtly hurt, nevertheless, by lighter trading [6] and hence fewer commissions for brokers, and by reduced profits or outright losses on stocks held by dealers.[7] This trouble for brokerage firms came on top of leftover problems from 1967 and 1968, particularly paperwork backlogs in "back offices." Many firms were forced to enlarge their staffs and invest heavily in automated record-keeping equipment.

When the profit-squeeze of 1969 came, several brokerage houses had to reduce their enlarged staffs and sometimes

[5] See *Congressional Quarterly Weekly Report*, Sept. 19, 1969, pp. 1720-1722.

[6] A record average of almost 13 million shares were traded daily in 1968 on the New York Stock Exchange and 8 million on the American Stock Exchange, compared with 11.3 million and 5.4 million, respectively, during the first seven months of 1969.

[7] Brokers and dealers often tend to be the same individual or firm. A broker handles the public's orders to buy and sell securities or commodities and charges a commission for this service. A dealer, typically, buys for his own account and sells to his own select customers. His profit or loss is the price difference.

45

close or consolidate branch offices. In a few instances, senior partners sold their prestigious seats on the New York Stock Exchange [8] to raise needed funds. *The Kiplinger Washington Letter* of Aug. 22, 1969, reported alarm in government "about the number of stockbrokers who are in a serious financial bind." There was fear of "a bad market scandal if one or two suddenly go broke."

' ' The brokerage firms' quest for capital turned in two main directions—that of "going public," selling stock in their own companies to the public, and that of raising commissions on trading of "odd lots," orders of less than 100 shares or $1,000 in value. Many brokerage houses have complained that it is becoming increasingly unprofitable to execute small orders.

Robert W. Haack, president of the New York Stock Exchange, has insisted that the small investor is not being shut óut of the market. "But to some extent," he acknowledges, "there has been a tendency by a relatively few brokerage firms to neglect him—to pay less attention to him." "It's a matter of pure economics," he added, "for a broker to try to make a big sale instead of a smaller one." [9] Wall Street writer Myron Kandel noted recently that only a few years ago, under the aegis of Haack's predecessor, Keith Funston, "the exchange vigorously promoted the concept of 'people's capitalism' and 'owning a share of America,' " but that "Now it is admitting that those little people it attracted to the stock market have not been getting the services they might have expected after heeding the call." [10]

"The past year," *Fortune* magazine commented in August 1969, "has brought a whole series of momentous happenings to the brokerage business, each suggesting that the industry is now enveloped by the changes it has so long resisted." The Board of Governors of the New York Stock Exchange moved on Sept. 18 to change its rules to allow member firms to "go public." It is expected on Wall Street that final approval by the Securities and Exchange Commission, and by the exchange's own membership, will come in time for some firms to take such action by Thanksgiving.

---

[8] At prices as low as $300,000 in August 1969, down from the record $515,000 apiece for two seats sold Jan. 2, 1969. A "seat" is owned by an individual, but his firm gains the right to trade on the exchange floor. Actual seats disappeared from the exchange in 1871 but the name remains to denote membership.

[9] Quoted in interview by *U. S. News & World Report*, Aug. 4, 1969, p. 63.

[10] Myron Kandel (editor of *Wall Street Letter*), in article for *Christian Science Monitor*, Aug. 30, 1969.

In fact, Donaldson, Lufkin & Jenrette, Inc., had gone so far—in defiance of exchange rules—as to register a stock offering with the S.E.C. on May 21, 1969.

Donaldson's initiative probably forced the exchange's hand, but many Wall Street observers had long felt that such a decision was inevitable. Only by public stock subscription, they reasoned, could a brokerage house obtain the capital needed to weather bad market years. If the rules change agreed to on Sept. 18 is finally sanctioned by the S.E.C. and the exchange membership, the directors of a stock exchange firm which goes public will have to be approved by the exchange's governors.

IMPACT OF INSTITUTIONAL FUNDS ON STOCK TRADING

The new rule will not open the doors of the exchange to insurance companies or similar large investors. The exchange will still require, as in the past, that a "primary purpose" of every exchange member must be "the transaction of business as a broker or dealer in securities." This requirement, however, may be less formidable as a barrier to membership by non-brokers than now appears, because antitrust action has been hinted by outsiders—on the ground that the present rule prevents securities customers from doing business directly rather than through a broker. If big institutional investors, such as insurance companies, handled their own brokerage business, it would mean the loss of lucrative commissions on Wall Street.

Antitrust action could threaten not only the composition of exchange membership but also the present system of fixing minimum brokerage fees. In hearings before the S.E.C. in April 1968, the Justice Department attacked the system, and on Jan. 17, 1969, its antitrust division filed a memorandum with the S.E.C. asking it to replace the existing system with one of negotiated fees. Richard W. McLaren, chief of the antitrust division in the Nixon administration, subsequently endorsed that view.

The S.E.C. is not expected to act on the fee question until it receives, perhaps early in 1970, the findings of a study now being conducted by the New York Stock Exchange. Haack indicated the direction the study had taken in letters he sent to member firms on Aug. 26, 1969. He said brokerage commissions were too high on very big orders and too low on very small ones. The timing of Haack's letter caused raised eyebrows at the S.E.C., as it was still at work on its own study. The S.E.C. in late 1968 had persuaded the exchanges and the over-the-counter market to reduce brokerage commissions on very large orders under an interim arrangement. But commissions were not reduced on small orders.

The impact of institutional investors on the stock market, already great, is a matter of concern to the S.E.C. At congressional direction, the agency in 1969 began a study of how institutional investments affect stock prices. The S.E.C. estimates that pension funds, mutual funds, insurance companies, trusts and the like account for about 50 per cent of the trading on the New York Stock Exchange. Commission studies indicate that these institutions purchased $38.2 billion in common stocks in 1968, surpassing the previous record of $27.7 billion in 1967. "Block trading," orders of 10,000 or more shares, increased greatly and at times was believed responsible for a wide price shift in the stock traded.[11]

Life insurance companies are the latest of the giants to enter the stock market. More than 100 life insurance companies or their affiliates became members of the National Association of Securities Dealers in 1968 in order to offer their policyholders an equity product—mutual funds or variable annuities. "The potential market awaiting the insurance company is astronomical," the association said in its 1968 annual report, "considering there are today only about five million people who own mutual funds as opposed to 150 million life insurance policyholders."

PAPERWORK BACKLOGS AND TRIALS OF AUTOMATION

Statistics such as these pour forth at a time when the stock market is only beginning to see daylight from beneath its paperwork problems. The prosperity that swamped brokerage houses in 1968 led increasingly to errors and "fails," the inability to complete a customer's order within five business days. A "fail" sets off a chain reaction in the market and costs the broker a penalty as well as loss of commission. The S.E.C., alarmed at the rising rate of fails,[12] prodded all

---

[11] See "Mutual Funds in the Market," *E.R.R.*, 1967 Vol. II, p. 537.

[12] On New York Stock Exchange trading in December 1968, fails occurred on transactions involving $4.1 billion in stocks, a record amount. The figure had declined to $1.4 billion by August 1969.

SHARES TRADED ON NEW YORK AND AMERICAN EXCHANGES

	Number of shares (in millions)		Per cent of U.S. total	
	NYSE	AMEX	NYSE	AMEX
1935	513.6	84.7	77.6	12.8
1945	496.0	152.4	66.6	20.5
1955	820.5	243.9	67.7	20.1
1965	1,809.4	582.2	69.9	22.5
1968	3,298.7	1,570.7	62.1	29.6

	Market value of shares (millions of dollars)		Per cent of U.S. total	
1935	$13,335	$1,205	87.3	7.9
1945	13,462	1,728	83.0	10.6
1955	32,745	2,593	86.5	6.8
1965	73,200	8,612	82.0	9.7
1968	144,978	34,775	73.8	17.7

SOURCE: Securities and Exchange Commission. Shares traded on the 11 smaller exchanges registered with S.E.C. aggregated 442.6 million in 1968, or 8.3% of the over-all total. Total value of shares traded on the smaller exchanges in 1968 amounted to $16.6 billion, or 8.5% of the over-all total.

exchanges and over-the-counter markets to close every Wednesday during the last half of 1968. They returned to a five-day week in 1969 but for shorter trading hours daily, currently from 10 A.M. to 3 P.M., 30 minutes earlier than the closing time in years past.

A few years ago, written complaints to the S.E.C. from stock customers could be numbered in hundreds. In 1968 the trickle turned into a flood, and by 1969 it was averaging 1,100 complaints a month. The volume of complaints was on a parallel line with trading volume in the stock market. For 39 years the busiest single day on the New York Stock Exchange had remained Oct. 29, 1929, the Black Tuesday which followed Black Thursday. On that day 16.4 million shares of stock changed hands. The 1929 peak was surpassed on 30 separate days in 1968, including June 13 when the all-time high of 21.3 million shares were traded.

There are reports almost everywhere that automated equipment is being perfected to relieve such problems as were encountered in 1968. But in the meantime there have been frustrations. The S.E.C. in February 1969 censured Lehman Brothers and all 39 of its general partners. The agency disclosed that at one time in May 1968 Lehman did not know to which of its numerous accounts some $473 million in securities should be allocated. The brokerage firm explained that a breakdown in its old-fashioned back-office bookkeeping had been compounded by an attempt to switch to automated record-keeping.

"Finding people who can master both machines and finance, either of which can be made into lifetime studies, remains a problem," a writer for the magazine *Finance* commented recently. Another reported that "If the market hadn't started declining, with a coincident dip in trading volume, the back-office situation today would be much worse than ever." [13] Much of the blame for the 1968 situation has been attributed to a forecast made by the New York Stock Exchange in December 1965—that only 10 million shares would be traded daily at the exchange by 1975.

Crash of 1929: Causes and Effects

THERE are parallels—and contrasts—between the stock market of 1929 and the market of 1969. The most obvious difference is that in 1969 there is government supervision of the stock market—a development that grew out of the 1929 crash. The most striking similarity might well be the pervasive economic optimism of the 1920s and the 1960s. It can be argued, and often is, whether the stock trader of the 1960s has become captivated by the same speculative fever as that which existed in the Twenties. Economic history can be read with an eye toward proving the safety, or danger, of stock investments in 1969. Whatever the comparisons or contrasts, an understanding of the development of the stock market in America is basic.

DEVELOPMENT OF STOCK MARKET; THE MORGAN ERA

To many people, the stock market means the New York Stock Exchange, an imposing structure with marble columns that stands at Wall and Broad Streets in lower Manhattan near the spot where George Washington took the oath of office as the nation's first President. It is the "Big Board," a name that reflects its dominance in stock trading.

But the Big Board did not always hold the dominant position. When the nation was young, and its political, economic and financial institutions were taking root, Philadel-

---

[13] The first quotation is from Robert L. Denerstein, "Wall Street's Frankenstein," *Finance*, July 1969, p. 36, and the second from S. M. Robards, "Fails—Dynamite in the Back Offices," *Finance*, March 1969, p. 53.

phia was the financial center of the country, just as it was the political capital until the seat of government was moved to Washington in 1800. In New York, a group of traders gathered daily next to a buttonwood tree on Wall Street to deal in government securities and bank stocks. In 1792, the traders banded together and signed the Buttonwood Tree Agreement, in which they pledged to trade only among themselves and charge outsiders a commission. The New York Stock Exchange traces its start to that agreement.

From those humble beginnings, the exchange kept pace with the growth of the nation whose expansion it helped to finance. It survived panics and booms, war and peace, crash and scandal. In 1863, its official name was changed to the New York Stock Exchange, and the end of the Civil War two years later opened up a period of unprecedented growth. The West was being settled, railroads were pushing into every corner of the country and large-scale manufacturing was taking hold.

Railroads needed large amounts of money to expand, and they found it convenient to place a great deal of power in the hands of bankers. In the depression years that followed in the 1870s, almost all of the railroads were in financial trouble and often the bankers gained control of them. Men like Edward H. Harriman, James J. Hill and William C. Whitney made fortunes in railroads while colorful figures like Jay Gould, Jim Fisk, Russell Sage, Commodore Cornelius Vanderbilt and Daniel Drew made and lost millions in speculation. The generation spanning the turn of the century produced leaders of giant corporations, like Andrew Carnegie, Charles Schwab and John D. Rockefeller.

The most powerful man of all in the American financial community was J. P. Morgan. His biographer, Lewis Corey, has described the House of Morgan [14] as being, as late as 1879, essentially an old-style financial institution, placing American securities in Europe, selling stocks and bonds and participating in government financing. "By 1889," Corey wrote, "the House of Morgan still did all these things, but in addition it participated directly in corporate affairs, combining, consolidating, centralizing, imposing the mastery of finance over industry." [15]

---

[14] J. Pierpont Morgan & Co. became Dabney, Morgan & Co. in 1863, then Drexel, Morgan & Co. in 1870, and J. P. Morgan & Co. in 1895.

[15] Lewis Corey, *House of Morgan* (1930), p. 132.

When Morgan took over a group of railroads or industrial companies, he would merge them, arrange extensive re-financing, and float new securities on the New York money market. The success of Morgan and his rivals depended on the market's ability to absorb new securities. A stock market panic in 1903 convinced the financiers that the small investor could not be relied upon, so they turned to trust and insurance companies for capital. The resulting Money Trust alarmed Progressives and became a target of reformers, including President Theodore Roosevelt. The trusts inspired the antitrust action which broke up the Standard Oil empire and whittled away at other combines. The elder J. P. Morgan died in 1913. His place was taken by his son, but a new era—the Age of the Great Bull Market—developed soon after World War I.

WALL STREET IN 1920S: THE GREAT BULL MARKET

Some students of the 1929 crash trace its origins to 1924 or 1927; others to 1921 or even 1914, the year World War I began in Europe. At the outset of war, America feared that Europeans would repatriate their business investments and leave this country's finances in shambles. Instead, foreign gold soon started arriving from Europe and by the war's end New York had replaced London as the foremost financial center of the world. Thus capital and a heady optimism, two essential ingredients for a rising stock market, were present in abundance. The sale of Liberty Bonds to pay for the American war effort in 1917-18 made masses of people securities owners for the first time—an experience that later led many of them into the stock market.

Stock prices rose during 1919 but then fell during the postwar depression of 1920-21. After this false start, the market in August 1921 began an upward surge that was to continue with only brief interruptions until the autumn of 1929. By 1924 the market advance embraced a wide range of stocks, and by 1927 the bull market entered its extravagant stage.

Unlike the bull market of 1919, the 1924-29 market was not accompanied by substantial increases in wholesale or retail prices. During the earlier boom, the stock advance reflected a general rise in prices. After 1924, however, prices of goods remained remarkably stable. By 1927 stock prices were rising even in the face of falling corporate earnings.

Most Americans in 1928 and 1929 were more interested in the stock market than in any other economic question. Writers of that era tell of waiters and chauffeurs eavesdropping to get market tips. For a few observers, interest was beginning to turn to concern. Early in 1929, the Federal Reserve Board, under continuing pressure from the New York Federal Reserve Bank, consented to warn member banks that they should not lend money for speculative purposes. However, the board could not agree until late summer to raise the "discount rate" on Fed lending to member banks from 5 per cent to 6 per cent. By then, brokers were paying banks interest rates as high as 12 per cent on money borrowed to finance customers' speculative stock buying on margin.[16] No specific margin was then required by law, and brokers generally asked a down payment of only 10 per cent of the purchase price in contrast to the 80 per cent now stipulated by the Federal Reserve Board.

By the summer of 1929 danger signs were beginning to show in business statistics. Starting in July, industrial production and employment fell off week after week. And prices dropped, except on the stock market. New York Stock Exchange averages reached record heights in early September. General Electric was up to 396, having tripled in price within 18 months. By early October, brokers' loans—an index of margin buying—topped $6 billion.

Added funds were supplied the market by investment trusts or investment companies, many of them sponsored by investment banks. These trusts pooled the resources of investors, mostly small investors, as is done today by mutual funds. The idea came from England and took root in this country in the 1920s amid public demand for stock ownership. Since a typical trust might hold securities in several hundred companies, a small investor could spread his risk.

OFFICIAL OPTIMISM IN FACE OF INEVITABLE CRASH

The New York Stock Exchange had an attack of nerves in early 1929. A market dip occurred in February; and a selling wave on March 26 made the day the busiest ever recorded until then. However, prices rebounded and investors

---

[16] When purchasing for a customer on margin, the broker buys the stock and pays for it in full but lends the customer a certain amount, holding the stock certificates as collateral. The difference between the amount loaned and the purchase price—the margin—is deposited by the customer to protect the broker against losses resulting from a decline in the price of the stock. In the late 1920s, 10 points was the amount of margin required by brokers on a majority of stocks. If the price fell close to or below that level, the customer had to put up additional margin or lose his stock.

had assurances that all was well. A few days before leaving office in March 1929, President Coolidge observed that the economy was "absolutely sound" and that stocks were "cheap at current prices." Bernard Baruch told Bruce Barton, in an interview published in the *American Magazine* in June, that "the economic condition of the world seems on the verge of a great forward movement." [17] Yale economist Irving Fisher was quoted as saying that autumn: "Stock prices have reached what looks like a permanently high plateau."

The bull market ended early in September, it is generally agreed now, but the turning point went unrecognized at the time. The market wavered unsteadily for a while and on Monday, Oct. 21, opened with a wave of selling—which Prof. Fisher considered "a shaking out of the lunatic fringe." Prices rallied in mid-week but on Thursday—Black Thursday, Oct. 24, 1929—prices broke sharply and selling reached a floodtide. In all, nearly 12.9 million shares changed hands, half again as many as ever before in a single day.

"In past panics," Prof. Robert Sobel has noted, "J. P. Morgan had taken charge, and his reputation and skill had stilled fears." [18] The elder Morgan was dead now and no one on Wall Street had his reputation or skill. However, the new leaders did try. A group of prominent bankers pooled several million dollars to bolster prices of key stocks. With this support, Exchange Vice President Richard Whitney rushed to the trading floor and conspicuously bid up the price of U. S. Steel. Instantly, those around him knew that a "bull pool" had been organized to stop the panic. Prices ebbed as trading ended that day and several prominent Americans, including President Hoover, had words of reassurance. "The fundamental business of the country . . . is on a sound and prosperous basis," Hoover said from the White House the next day.

But by the following Monday, stock prices sagged again and investors soon gave in to fright and confusion. From the moment the New York Stock Exchange opened Tuesday morning—Black Tuesday, Oct. 29—it was besieged by frantic

---

[17] Baruch, recording in his autobiography "my own feelings in those days," said: "From 1928 on, I felt uneasy about the level of stock prices. Looking out over world affairs, I could see where a new surge of prosperity might be touched off if we could solve the problem of reparations and war debts. . . . On the other hand, I did not like the effects of the loosening of credit that the Federal Reserve had begun in 1927. . . . Soon after I landed in New York [after a trip abroad in the late summer of 1929], I decided to sell everything I could."—*Baruch, My Own Story* (1957), pp. 243-244.

[18] Robert Sobel, *The Great Bull Market* (1968), p. 135.

efforts to sell at any price. The day was the most disastrous in the history of the exchange, eclipsing Black Thusday in terms of statistics: 16.4 million shares were traded, and untold losses incurred.

POST-MORTEMS ON 1929 CRASH AND THE DEPRESSION

The day would become legendary, giving rise to endless tales—many false—of instant bankruptcy and even suicide. Bad as it was, the crash was not then accorded the significance it has since assumed. The *New York Times* editors did not consider it the biggest news story of the year; that honor went to Adm. Richard E. Byrd's expedition to Antarctica. There was some recovery in the stock market in the early months of 1930 but none after May of that year. By the end of 1930 there was no doubt that the nation was in a depression.

Even today there is no agreement among students of the crash whether it caused the depression. "The causes of the Great Depression are still far from certain," John Kenneth Galbraith has written. "Cause and effect run from the economy to the stock market, never in reverse." [19] Prof. Sobel holds that "No causal relationship between the events of late October 1929 and the Great Depression has ever been shown through the use of empirical evidence." [20] But Arthur M. Schlesinger Jr. maintains that "by shattering confidence, the crash knocked out any hope of automatic recovery in the economy as a whole." [21] Galbraith tends to see the 1920s as an inexorable march toward disaster. In contrast, Sobel argues that "The crash did not seem inevitable to Americans of 1929." He believes that "Most of today's investors, faced with the kind of market which existed in 1929, would more than likely have been bulls rather than bears."

Regulation of the Securities Business

THE STOCK MARKET CRASH of 1929 led to government supervision of the securities business—but not immediately. It was a delayed reaction. President Hoover favored self-regulation but indicated a willingness to accept new legislation if Wall Street did not reform itself. Although the New

[19] John Kenneth Galbraith, *The Great Crash* (1955), p. 176.
[20] Robert Sobel, *op. cit.*, p. 147.
[21] Arthur M. Schlesinger Jr., *The Crisis of the Old Order* (1956), p. 160.

York Stock Exchange took a few hesitant steps, its members clung to the view that Congress had "no more constitutional authority to lay down rules for the conduct of their business than to regulate the affairs of a private club." [22]

The Democratic platform of 1932 advocated regulation of the exchanges. However, the party's presidential candidate, Franklin D. Roosevelt, took no firm stand on the question until after he was elected. By then, a Senate subcommittee, with Ferdinand Pecora as its counsel, had begun an investigation which for the next two years would reveal duplicity and fraud in the stock market both before and after the 1929 crash. [23] The subcommittee hearings are perhaps best remembered now for the press agent's stunt of posing a midget on the knee of J. P. Morgan Jr. as he prepared to testify in 1933. It was those hearings, however, that created the climate in Congress for enactment of the Securities Act of 1933 and the Securities Exchange Act of 1934—which remain the two basic laws regulating the securities business.

The Securities and Exchange Commission, created by the 1934 law, was authorized to guard the public interest in stock and bond dealings. The Securities Act of 1933 required registration of securities publicly offered for sale in interstate commerce or through the mails and a "full and fair" disclosure of all pertinent facts. The government was not to pass on the merits of the securities; they could be offered for sale regardless of their worth if the truth was told.

The Securities Exchange Act of 1934 attempted to prevent the manipulation of securities that were already on the market prior to enactment of the 1933 law and hence not subject to its regulation. The 1934 act had other broad regulatory features, including that of requiring stock exchanges [24] to enforce compliance with S.E.C. rules by their member firms.

James M. Landis was given the job of policing the securities business under the auspices of the Federal Trade Commission until the new S.E.C. was ready to function, Sept. 1, 1934. It was widely assumed that Landis, a former dean of

---

[22] See "Stock Exchanges and Security Speculation," *E.R.R.*, 1930 Vol. I, pp. 75-94, and "The Federal Reserve System and Stock Speculation," *E.R.R.*, 1929 Vol. II, pp. 425-444.

[23] See Senate *Subcommittee on Banking and Currency: Stock Exchange Hearings Practices, 1932-34.*

[24] They numbered 19 in 1934. Today 13 are registered with the S.E.C. They are the New York Stock Exchange, American, Boston, Chicago Board of Trade, Cincinnati, Detroit, Midwest, National, Pacific Coast, Philadelphia-Baltimore-Washington, Pittsburgh, Salt Lake City and Spokane.

the Harvard Law School whom Wall Street considered a radical, would become the commission's first chairman. "Perhaps realizing that the establishment of the S.E.C. had alienated financial leaders," Prof. Sobel has written, "Roosevelt made a characteristic gesture of compromise; he named Joseph Kennedy as Chairman in a move that stunned both Wall Street and New Dealers."

> Landis protested bitterly; legislative committees had just finished examining Kennedy's manipulations . . . and although he was not guilty of legal crimes, the morality of his action was questionable. Ironically, the new S.E.C. would be headed by a man who symbolized the kind of Wall Streeter the Commission was designed to curb! [25]

But Joseph P. Kennedy, father of a future President, is judged to have done a good job in getting the commission on its feet, and he soothed the financial community with his moderate interpretation of S.E.C. powers. The truce between Washington and Wall Street was short-lived, nonetheless. Landis became chairman when Kennedy resigned in 1935, and Landis in turn was replaced by William O. Douglas in 1937. Landis and Douglas pressed the Big Board to correct "serious defects"; Douglas, especially, attacked the "private club" character of the exchange.

Richard Whitney, the hero of Black Thursday 1929 who was now president of the exchange, rallied the opposition—until March 1938 when it was disclosed that he had embezzled and run his brokerage firm into bankruptcy. A biographer describes Whitney as one of the most admired men on Wall Street—"The scion of seventeenth-century Massachusetts settlers . . . the son of a Boston bank president, and the nephew of a former Morgan partner. At Groton School . . . decades later he was still a well-remembered favorite of the Reverend Endicott Peabody." [26] Whitney's fall dissolved resistance to change at the New York Stock Exchange; in April 1938 the exchange adopted a new constitution and the following October its new board of governors approved a set of Douglas's reform proposals.

Self-Regulation in the Over-the-Counter Market

Making the exchanges conduct their business to its satisfaction is only part of the S.E.C.'s task. The other, and equally difficult, part entails over-the-counter trading. The

---

[25] Robert Sobel, *op. cit.*, *The Big Board* (1965), p. 300.
[26] John Brooks, *Once in Golconda* (1969), p. 61.

O-T-C market is so diffuse—it encompasses brokerage businesses across the nation—that it presents regulatory problems unknown to the exchanges. Under terms of the Maloney
Amendment of 1938 (to the 1934 law), the National Association of Securities Dealers was created in 1939 to exercise
a degree of self-policing in such trading.[27] But the S.E.C.
still complained in its 10th annual report, in 1944, that there
was "substantial evidence that the number as well as the
importance of unregistered securities dealt in in the over-
the-counter market has increased in recent years."

Over-the-counter stocks typically are in companies that
are small, new, and full of growth potential. These stocks
usually are modestly priced in keeping with their low or
non-existent profits. The small investor can purchase enough
shares to make a real killing if the stock takes off. But the
risks are great, too. In recent months O-T-C stocks have
tended to suffer greater losses than those sold on the exchanges, and a bad recession might endanger some of the
small companies.

Congress in 1968 gave the Federal Reserve Board the
same legal authority to set margin requirements on O-T-C
stocks as the board had possessed since 1934 with regard to
stocks sold on the exchanges. For the first time, on July 8,
1969, the board subjected 290 O-T-C stocks to the current
margin requirement—80 per cent. The "Fed" deemed the
290 active enough nationally to warrant this action.

The National Quotation Bureau in New York lists about
8,000 O-T-C securities. N.A.S.D. estimates there are about
30,000 securities in all, but an association official, Ralph
Burgess, acknowledges that no one knows with any degree
of precision. The association hopes to learn more about the
size of the market in March or April 1970 from a canvass
of financial reports from brokers and dealers. Even then,
the picture will not be complete because some persons who
sell stocks in-state only are exempt.

Congress, S.E.C., and New Securities Legislation

Congress has perhaps shown more concern over the securities markets in the 1960s than at any time since the
1930s. The S.E.C. in 1963 published what is known as the
Special Study of the Securities Market, the most exhaustive
survey of its kind in three decades. From the study, under-

---

[27] See "Protection of Investors," *E.R.R.*, 1955 Vol. I, pp. 53-56.

taken at congressional direction, came the Securities Acts Amendments of 1964, which extended many areas of investor protection to the over-the-counter markets and elevated the standards of training for dealers and brokers.

But Congress is not always amenable to S.E.C. legislative proposals. In 1967 after lengthy studies [28] the commission asked Congress for legislation to tighten controls over mutual fund companies and reduce costs to investors. The Senate approved a bill in 1968 that hewed close to the S.E.C. proposals, but it died in the House Commerce Committee when the 90th Congress ended. A bill intended as a compromise to meet objections of the mutual fund companies was introduced in 1969 and by October had won Senate, but not House, passage. [29]

NIXON'S VIEWS; CRITICISM OF NEW S.E.C. CHAIRMAN

The relations of the S.E.C. with Wall Street were often chilly during the years (1964-Feb. 22, 1969) when Manuel F. (Manny) Cohen was commission chairman. A member of the agency for 29 years, and a commissioner for eight, Cohen was known as a tough regulator. A warming trend thus was freely predicted when Richard M. Nixon became President. As a candidate in September 1968, Nixon had circulated among 3,000 financial executives a letter criticizing the "heavy-handed bureaucratic regulatory schemes" of the Johnson administration. The following month, in response to written questions submitted by the *Los Angeles Times*, he vowed that as President he would seek, through appointment of new officials to regulatory agencies, to reduce the level of government controls over business. [30]

There was published speculation late in 1968 that, under a Republican majority, the S.E.C. would soften its views on an issue especially troublesome on Wall Street and in executive suites—what constitutes *inside* information concerning stocks. S.E.C. lawyers had argued in a celebrated case involving the Texas Gulf Sulphur Co. [31] that an insider includes

[28] *The Wharton School Study of Mutual Funds* (1962), conducted for the S.E.C., and the commission's own report to Congress in 1966 on *Public Policy Implications of Investment Company Growth*. See "Mutual Funds in the Market," *E.R.R.*, 1967 Vol. II, pp. 539-556.

[29] See *Congressional Quarterly Weekly Report*, May 30, 1969, pp. 879-880, and CQ 1968 *Almanac*, p. 665.

[30] See "Federal Regulatory Agencies: Fourth Branch of Government," *E.R.R.*, 1969 Vol. I, pp. 85-100.

[31] The S.E.C. in 1965 accused Texas Gulf officials of benefiting from inside information about an oil strike in Canada and deliberately trying to mislead the public about it. A U.S. Court of Appeals in 1968 reversed the trial court judgment on several major points and upheld the S.E.C. views.

not only officers, directors and major stockholders of a corporation, but also almost anyone who, by virtue of his relationship with the company, has access to confidential information about it. Federal law prohibits insiders from trading on such information until it has been made public.

Hamer H. Budge, whom Nixon elevated to the S.E.C. chairmanship on Feb. 22, had supported S.E.C. action in a series of insider cases during his service as a member of the commission since 1964. While a member of Congress (1951-61), Budge was considered a political conservative. But the *Wall Street Journal* commented, May 1, 1969, that his conservatism did not signify someone who was "soft on business and strong on laissez faire philosophy." The newspaper considered him a "strict constructionist" who would insist that securities laws be enforced but not widened by interpretation, as Cohen was sometimes accused of doing. In one of his few recent speeches, an address before executives of the Association of Stock Exchange Firms, Budge stressed self-regulation. The *New York Times* reported the next day, Sept. 5, 1969, that the speech was being interpreted in Manhattan as "tantamount to proffering an olive branch to Wall Street."

Eliot Janeway, who looks at economic events in historical perspective, places less stress on Washington-Wall Street relations than on White House-Capitol Hill relations. "When the President and the Congress work in harmony together, . . . no negative pressures to which the stock market is subjected can keep it down," Janeway believes. "Contrariwise, when a breach develops between the President and Congress . . . no expansive pressures which conventional analysis identifies as constructive can hold the stock market up." [32]

Almost every man on Wall Street has expounded his own ideas about stock market movement, but none has been persuasive enough to win more than a handful of converts. Until the currents of the stock market are identified in the making with greater precision, hindsight will continue to serve as the only firm guide. It is the investor's hope that the hindsight offered by the 1929 crash will be sufficient to avert any comparable upheaval in the 1970s.

---

[32] Eliot Janeway, "Politics and the Stock Market," *The Anatomy of Wall Street* (1967), p. 205.

PRIVATE HOUSING SQUEEZE

by

Hoyt Gimlin

1 9 6 9
July 9

PRIVATE HOUSING SQUEEZE

EVERY AMERICAN not sunk in poverty has assumed for a quarter-century or more that he could buy a house, if he so chose, as often as he moved. And that is often, because the Census Bureau reports that one American family in five changes its place of residence every year. For some time now, however, those who still clung to the notion of easy access to home ownership have been in for a rude awakening.

"The single-family home is moving into the category of a luxury item," a New Jersey builder said recently. "In the market where our company is building today—and it's typical in this regard—a family must have close to a $14,000 income to be able to buy a home." [1]

Housing agencies have reported that on-site houses selling for less than $15,000 made up only 8 per cent of the single-family housing market in 1968, while five years earlier they accounted for 29 per cent. Seventy per cent of new houses sold during 1968 were priced above $20,000, and the median price for older houses rose—for the first time—above $20,000.

TIGHT MONEY SUPPLY AND HIGH INTEREST RATES

The cost of housing continued to rise during the first half of 1969, with no slackening in sight. Higher prices for land, lumber, labor and capital all showed up in new mortgages. Persons who could afford to do so were willing to pay the prices. But by the summer of 1969, money for home building was diminishing under the impact of monetary restraints imposed to slow down the worst inflation since 1951. The scarcity of lending funds was reminding builders and bankers of the now-famous "credit crunch" of 1966. [2]

Mortgage interest rates reached record heights in 1969, standing at a national average of 7.64 per cent in May on "conventional" loans—those that are not insured by the Fed-

---

[1] Robert H. Winnerman, board chairman of U. S. Home & Development Corp., quoted by *Washington Post*, June 28, 1969.

[2] See "Money Supply in Inflation," *E.R.R.*, 1969 Vol. I, pp. 145-161.

eral Housing Administration or the Veterans Administration. Conventional loans account for about four-fifths of the market. The latest monthly figure on interest rates for such loans, reported by the Federal Home Loan Bank Board, was almost a full percentage point higher than a year earlier. The United States Savings and Loan League reported that interest rates on new mortgages ranged from 6.88 to 8.03 per cent. The effective rate was probably higher because the borrower, to obtain financing, may have had to pay "points" —the trade name for the legally permissible practice of discounting the face value of a loan. Points have the effect of making the interest rate higher than stated in the mortgage contract.[3]

Interest rates in May did not reflect the latest rise in the "prime rate" of interest which big city banks charge favored borrowers—others pay more. The "prime rate" was raised a full percentage point on June 9 to a record 8½ per cent. "A one-point increase in the [mortgage] interest rate," George Romney, Secretary of Housing and Urban Development, said two days later, "causes a 7 per cent to 10 per cent increase in the cost of housing."

Mortgage interest rates to individuals may actually be less than the prime rate. The big New York banks changed the prime rate to deter massive business borrowing but did not change their mortgage rates. However, an increase in the prime rate tends to bring about an increase in various other interest rates and thus have the effect of draining money away from the principal sources of mortgage funds: savings and loan associations and insurance companies. Savers tend to put their money in bonds or other high-yield investments, and policyholders borrow on their life insurance at rates of 4 or 5 per cent because it is cheaper than borrowing from other sources. The result is to leave savings institutions and insurance companies with fewer funds for mortgage lending.

The government has moved, with some success, to offset these factors. One of Secretary Romney's first acts upon assuming office last January was to raise the interest ceiling on government-backed mortgages to 7½ per cent up from 6¾ per cent, thus making the guaranteed mortgages a more

---

[3] A point is one per cent of the loan. If the borrower pays four points on a $20,000 loan, he actually receives only $19,200 (4 per cent of $20,000 is $800). But he pays interest on the full $20,000. On a 20-year mortgage at 7 per cent interest, the effective rate actually becomes 7.53 per cent.

Private Housing Squeeze

PRIVATE HOUSING STARTS, 1946-67

Year	Total*	% Conventional	% F.H.A.	% V.A.
1946	1,015.2	84.4	6.6	9.0
1949	1,429.8	76.0	17.7	6.3
1952	1,445.4	74.4	15.8	9.8
1955†	1,626.6	59.3	16.5	24.2
1958	1,134.2	71.6	20.6	7.8
1961	1,284.8	88.0	15.5	6.5
1962	1,439.0	80.9	13.7	5.4
1963	1,582.9	85.0	10.5	4.5
1964	1,502.3	85.9	10.2	3.9
1965	1,450.6	85.6	11.0	3.4
1966	1,141.5	85.5	11.3	3.2
1967	1,268.4	84.7	11.2	5.1
Totals, 1946-67	30,596.0‡	76.0	14.6	9.4

* In thousands of units (does not include mobile homes).
† All-time peak.
‡ 1968 total: 1,507.7 (breakdown not available).
SOURCE: Economic Report of the President, January 1969, p. 275.

attractive investment. Some states elevated permissible rates under their usury laws to 8 per cent and beyond. The government-chartered Federal National Mortgage Association ("Fannie Mae") has been issuing short- and medium-term securities to pump a recent average of $100 million a week into the mortgage market.[4]

TREND FROM PRIVATE DWELLINGS TO APARTMENTS

The Commerce Department reported that new construction of private housing declined in May 1969, for the fourth straight month, to an annual rate slightly below that for 1968 when housing starts totaled 1.5 million units. Current forecasts project a continued decline through the summer and fall, resulting in an annual output 200,000 units or so under the previous year's total—but still more than the 1.1 million units started during 1966. In that year, as in 1969, the housing market suffered from the anti-inflationary tight money policies imposed by the Federal Reserve Board.

The true extent of the decline in single-family housing is "camouflaged," according to Tom B. Scott Jr., president of the United States Savings and Loan League, because the official figures include apartment construction. Apartment units accounted for only 35 per cent of all housing starts in

---

[4] F.N.M.A. does for mortgages guaranteed by F.H.A. and V.A. what the Federal Land Bank system does for conventionally financed mortgages. It purchases mortgages in areas where there is a shortage of real-estate capital, and sells them in areas where there is a surplus of savings. The mortgages are purchased with government funds.

1965, but their share rose to 40 per cent in 1968 and then mounted to one-half of all units in January 1969 and to two-thirds in April. John A. Stasny, vice president-treasurer of the National Association of Home Builders, recently called this increase a "remarkable shift to apartment building and financing." [5]

Economic columnist Joseph R. Slevin asserted early in April that "Builders of large apartment houses . . . can get mortgage loans, for many are willing to give a big lender, such as an insurance company, an equity 'kicker' that guarantees the lender a share of the profits." Lenders have their pick of investments, Slevin said, "and are cold-shouldering conventional mortgages that only pay interest and do not cut them into the builder's profits." [6] "Americans may become increasingly a nation of apartment dwellers—out of sheer necessity," Thomas W. Bush of the *Los Angeles Times* observed May 18, 1969, in reporting on the high cost of West Coast housing.

The movement of urban Americans into apartments is not necessarily to be deplored, in the opinion of many critics of low-density suburbs. They see the vast expanses of single-family housing in suburbia as a misuse of land that breeds urban sprawl, commuter problems, and numerous other metropolitan ills. Whether good or bad, the proliferation of single-family homes on the fringes of big cities has been taken for granted for decades. If the time has come for urbanites and suburbanites both to change their living habits, as is perhaps evidenced by the rising of apartment towers on more and more suburban landscapes, it is clear that the housing problem is no longer confined to inner-city slums. It is moving out to the encircling suburbs.

SLIPPAGE IN PROGRESS TOWARD HOUSING GOALS

The total of 1.5 million new housing starts attained in 1968, despite mounting costs, was the largest recorded in any year since 1963. But the total was well below goals fixed by Congress in the Housing and Urban Development Act of 1968. That act set forth a policy of striving for 26 million units of new or rehabilitated housing within 10 years—an average of 2.6 million a year. Congress was reaffirming what it had said in the National Housing Act of 1949, that "a

---

[5] Statements by Scott and Stasny at convention of National Association of Mutual Savings Banks, Minneapolis, May 27, 1969.

[6] Column in *Washington Post*, April 6, 1969.

decent home and a suitable living environment for every American family" was the ultimate objective.

That objective is still elusive. In 1968, almost two decades after the goal was first set, the National Advisory Commission on Civil Disorders reported that inadequate housing was a major complaint among residents of almost every area in which riots had occurred. Congress pointed out in its policy declaration in the 1968 act that the 1949 goal "has not been realized for many of the nation's lower-income families; that this is a matter of grave national concern; and that there exist in the public and private sectors of the economy the resources and capabilities necessary to the full realization of this goal." But on May 8, 1969, Secretary Romney told a news conference: "We are falling behind every day at the present rate of production." The Secretary thereupon announced "Operation Breakthrough," a $20 million project to promote new ways of building cheaper housing. One of the ways would be to adapt assembly-line techniques—especially those used by makers of mobile homes—to the building of on-site housing.

INCREASES IN COSTS OF LUMBER, LAND AND LABOR

"The cost of housing," Romney noted at his May 8 news conference, "has gone up faster than the cost of other things that a family buys." Consumer prices, as recorded by the Bureau of Labor Statistics, rose 6.9 per cent between January 1968 and May 1969; housing, as one element of the consumer price index, rose 7.6 per cent during that 16-month period. The index reflected higher rentals and, for the home owner, higher mortgage interest, property taxes, insurance, and maintenance and repair costs.

Another official price index, that for wholesale commodities, recorded a spectacular rise during 1968 in the cost of lumber—a principal house-building material. The entire index went up only 2.1 per cent, but construction materials in general climbed 9.1 per cent, and lumber and wood products jumped 24.7 per cent. Among wood products, prices of plywood soared 50.3 per cent during the year—one type of plywood 91.8 per cent, almost doubling in price. The cost of lumber and wood products continued to increase through April 1969 but then sagged; by June it had dropped to a five-year low—a reflection of declining construction activity. Industry officials predicted that lumber prices would go up again if the building boom resumed.

The Senate Subcommittee on Housing and Urban Affairs, a unit of the Banking and Currency Committee, held hearings March 19-21, 1969, into lumber pricing and production. They produced a picture of lumber shortages in 1968 resulting from a combination of bad logging weather in the Pacific Northwest during the winter of 1967-68, a rising volume of exports to Japan, an unexpectedly heavy demand from American builders,[7] and a shortage of railroad freight cars to ship lumber to the East Coast.

Romney testified that after-tax profits of the lumber industry rose from 8.6 per cent for the year 1967 to 16.3 per cent for the third quarter of 1968, the latest period for which figures were available.[8] The Secretary declined to say, under questioning by Sen. William Proxmire (D Wis.) and other subcommittee members, whether he considered the profits excessive. He did express concern that "If lumber prices keep on going up, . . . other raw material producers are going to take a look at it and may be influenced by it."

In its defense, the industry said that lumber and wood products accounted for only about 20 per cent of the construction cost of a single-family dwelling, and for about 10 per cent of the selling price. "Obviously, lumber price increases alone could not have catapulted housing costs by more than 40 per cent since 1957-59," a spokesman said. "The cost of almost everything else that goes into a house has risen, too: Building lot prices are 80 per cent above the 1957-59 level, labor costs are up more than 50 per cent, construction machinery and equipment has climbed nearly 30 per cent."[9]

Others have calculated that for detached single-family houses, the structure itself accounts for only 40 to 60 per cent of the total price. The cost of land, site improvements marketing and financing take up the remainder. Land costs have been the biggest single factor in the rising cost of housing since World War II, the National Commission on Urban Problems headed by former Sen. Paul H. Douglas (D Ill.), said May 6, 1969, in its final report.[10]

---

[7] Lumber consumption in the United States during 1968 amounted to 42.1 billion board-feet, some 2.5 billion more than in 1967. Softwoods accounted for more than four-fifths of the total, and housing for abut 40-50 per cent of the softwoods.

[8] After-tax profits stated as a percentage return on investment. Comparable figures for all manufacturing were 11.7 per cent for 1967 and 11.4 per cent for the third quarter of 1968.

[9] Ernest J. Hodges, president of American Forest Institute, in statement in June 1969.

[10] *U. S. Land Prices—Directions and Dynamics: Research Report No. 13*. President Johnson appointed the commission Jan. 12, 1967, to conduct a study, ordered by Congress in 1965, of building and housing codes, zoning, tax policies and development standards.

Another study group, the President's Committee on Urban Housing, reported in December 1968 that land today accounts, on a national average, for 20 per cent of the total cost of housing, varying from 11 per cent in Idaho to 40 per cent in Hawaii. According to a study conducted for the committee by the McGraw-Hill Co., the price of "raw land" doubled in major metropolitan areas between 1950 and 1965; in some places of especially rapid growth, like Staten Island, N. Y., and Montgomery County, Md., it went up fivefold.

Labor unions have been widely blamed for their part in pushing up the cost of housing. It is asserted (1) that some of their recent wage increases have been inflationary; (2) that they veto labor-saving and cost-saving innovations; and (3) that restrictive membership practices keep the manpower in their crafts in short supply. Secretary Romney cited statistics in May 1969 showing that the average wage increase in construction-union settlements was almost 50¢ an hour ($20 per 40-hour week) in 1968, four times as much as in 1962. "There is every indication future settlements will be higher," he told a meeting of the AFL-CIO Building and Construction Trades Department, to the accompaniment of lusty cheers. He had been booed by the same audience moments earlier for saying that housing costs were "the biggest cause of inflation" and that higher labor costs were partly responsible.

Government Aid to Private Housing

IN THIS COUNTRY the tradition of private ownership of property—including home ownership—is long and strong. Property owners wrote the laws of the new nation and dominated its social thinking. Thomas Jefferson extolled the virtues of yeoman farmers who were beholden to no landlord. To Americans, the word "renters" often conveyed the image of impermanent and perhaps impoverished people.

Until the Great Depression of the 1930s, house building and house buying were considered the exclusive province of private enterprise. "The New Deal venture into realty operations was a striking departure from traditional boundaries of federal power," Charles Abrams has written. "The prevailing American attitude after the First World War, when England launched a government-subsidized housing program, was that private initiative was not only to play first fiddle but call the tune and pull the strings." [11]

Money lenders charged high interest rates, required large down payments and rapid repayment on mortgage loans, typically 35 per cent initially and the remainder within seven to 10 years. Periodic payments often covered only the interest, with the full principal due at the expiration date. Buyers who could not meet a payment because of illness or loss of a job were in danger of forfeiting their homes and all the savings invested in them. In that setting, money lenders were frequently portrayed as villains in plays and novels, and the mortgage evoked a sense of fear.

The prosperity of the 1920s tended to hide these risks. Home ownership increased substantially at the same time that values became highly inflated. After the economy started to slide in 1929, millions lost their homes by foreclosure and the threat of foreclosure hung over millions of others. In 1934, when recovery had barely set in, housing starts numbered only 90,000 units, one-tenth the annual average of the 1920s.

INITIATION OF FEDERAL HOUSING AID IN DEPRESSION

The depression brought the federal government into the housing picture. First, under President Hoover, the Federal Home Loan Banks were set up to supply capital advances to savings and home-financing institutions. In the Roosevelt administration, the Home Owners Loan Corporation was created to stem continuing defaults. The latter agency made long-term mortgage loans, at low interest rates, directly to individuals in urgent need of funds to retain or recover ownership of their homes and unable to obtain normal financing for that purpose. Also in the mid-1930s, the government undertook to insure deposits in federally chartered savings and loan associations. Mortgage lenders in general did away with "balloon payments" at the end of the mortgage term by amortizing the principal in regular payments over the life of the loan. Interest rates were reduced.

Both the home owner and the lender were aided by these government measures and by the reforms they promoted.

---

[11] Charles Abrams, "The Future of Housing," *Urban Renewal: People, Politics and Planning* (1967), p. 37.

"Strangely," the National (Douglas) Commission on Urban Problems has observed, "the same economic middle class which then received these benefits and in large measure still does, often forgets its debt to society; many of its members are frequently in the forefront of opposition to housing programs designed to help less fortunate Americans." [12]

While the government kept a significant number of Americans from losing their homes, the hoped-for recovery of the housing market did not occur. Financial institutions that handled the mortgages were stabilized, but they were still fearful of making home loans for which they might not be repaid. In 1935 the Federal Housing Administration was created to insure mortgages extended to home owners by lending institutions. If the home owner failed to make his payments, he was not bailed out—he lost his home. The guarantee was given to the lender, assuring him of repayment even if the borrower defaulted.[13] This arrangement enabled the lender to make virtually risk-free loans on new and used homes, and on home repair work when covered by F.H.A. guarantees. The lender, in turn, was willing to accept low down payments and long-term mortgages, currently up to 35 years. Thus the borrower with little capital was able to find financing.

F.H.A. AND V.A. ASSISTANCE IN POSTWAR PERIOD

Congress in 1944 and 1945 provided similar home-buying assistance to returning veterans of World War II, later extended to Korean War and Viet Nam veterans. In all, about 6.8 million veterans have taken advantage of housing features of the various GI Bills administered by the Veterans Administration. V.A. insurance covered losses up to 60 per cent of the amount of the mortgage loan, subject originally to a maximum cost to the V.A. of $7,500. In the early days of the program this ceiling was ample, because it was unusual for a veteran's house to cost more than $12,000. Veterans financing virtually eliminated down payments and probably reached farther down the income scale than the F.H.A., which required fixed percentages. More than one-half of the home buyers who received V.A. assistance had incomes of $4,800 to $7,200. However, persons at this income level had been largely priced out of the market in 1969. Congress rec-

---

[12] *Building the American City* (December 1968), p. 94.

[13] Repayment is made from an insurance fund which is financed by the addition of one-half of one per cent to mortgage interest rates.

ognized in 1968 that the $7,500 ceiling was no longer realistic and raised it to $12,500.

From 1946 through 1967, F.H.A.-insured mortgages financed 4.4 million units of new housing, and V.A.-insured mortgages 2.9 million units. Together, they helped to finance almost one-fourth of all private housing built since World War II.

STRENGTH AND WEAKNESS OF THE F.H.A. PROGRAM

"It is difficult to see how any institution could have served the emerging middle class more effectively than has the F.H.A. and its counterpart, the Federal Home Loan Bank System," the Douglas commission observed. "The main weakness of the F.H.A. from a social point of view has not been in what it has done, but in what it has failed to do—its relative neglect of the inner cities and of the poor, especially the Negro poor."

> Believing that the poor were bad credit risks and that the presence of Negroes tended to lower real estate values, F.H.A. has generally regarded loans to such groups as "economically unsound." . . . The poor and those on the fringes of poverty have been almost completely excluded. These and the lower middle class, together constituting 40 per cent of the population whose housing needs are the greatest, received only 11 per cent of F.H.A. mortgages.[14]

Yet, the commission noted, F.H.A. had a strong case for its economic conservatism. Under public and congressional criticism, the agency began relaxing some of its rules in the 1960s. Defaults rose from an average rate of 0.9 per cent in 1960 to 3.7 per cent in 1967. Not all of the difference could be attributed to the new marginal groups of home buyers, but it alarmed some members of Congress sufficiently to demand greater caution. On the other hand, congressional liberals, seeing the deterioration of the central cities, wanted F.H.A. to take more chances and help rebuild at least the "gray fringes" of the central cities.[15]

Congress in 1968 acted to clear up some doubt about its intent. In section 102 of the 1968 Housing Act, it authorized F.H.A. to insure loans to families with low and moderate incomes who could not qualify under the old housing programs because of past credit ratings or of irregularities of income. Preference was given to prospective home owners

---

[14] National Commission on Urban Problems, *Building the American City* (1968), p. 100.
[15] See "Housing for the Poor," *E.R.R.*, 1966 Vol. I, pp. 163-179.

among (1) families living in public housing, (2) especially those forced to leave because their incomes had risen above levels prescribed by local housing authorities, and (3) those who were eligible for public housing and had been displaced by urban renewal. The law further authorized F.H.A. to insure mortgages which would permit the repair, construction or purchase of properties in older and declining urban areas which could not normally meet all the eligibility requirements because of the nature of their surroundings.

Barriers to Mass-Housing Technology

THE HOME is the most costly possession of most Americans and one of their basic symbols of status. Broadly defined, housing is the foremost consumer good in the United States. Americans spend more than $100 billion annually to buy, rent, operate and maintain their living places. Roughly 10 per cent of the Gross National Product each year is devoted to construction of all kinds; residential buildings account for about one-third of that amount. The President's Committee on Urban Housing, headed by industrialist Edgar F. Kaiser, has estimated that consumers would have $1 billion for every decrease of 1 per cent in the cost of owning, renting and operating their residences.

But few savings are likely, barring a breakthrough in housing technology and a change of laws and attitudes which so far have inhibited major innovation in the field. "As a people who are, for the most part, socially and economically mobile," Robert C. Weaver has said, "we have a tendency to accept the established, to question the novel, and to resist the unknown. For mobility creates insecurity, and insecurity breeds conservatism. Nowhere is this more apparent than in shelter. . . . The building industry and financial institutions, partly because of these tendencies and partly because of their own conservatism, develop an inertia against innovation." [16]

Home building in the United States is a fragmented, handcrafted trade that has been unable or unwilling to adopt assembly-line practices. There is no General Motors of hous-

---

[16] Robert C. Weaver (former HUD Secretary), *Dilemmas of Urban America* (1965), p. 9. Weaver's book is based on the Godkin lectures he delivered at Harvard in March 1965.

ing, as critics have repeated for years in portraying housing as a laggard in the industrial 20th century. No name in the home-building industry, except perhaps that of William B. Levitt, the mass developer of Levittowns, is widely known.

For the most part, the industry is a collection of small contractors who come together on a project-by-project basis. The Douglas commission counted some 322,781 firms engaged in contract construction. Fewer than one-half of them had four employees or more; only 10 per cent had 20 or more. The National Association of Home Builders reported in 1964 that a survey of its member-builders showed that their average individual production was 49 single-family houses a year.

"If the production of automobiles in the United States were as primitive as the production of urban housing," Walter McQuade of *Fortune* wrote recently, "the customer would go to his local service station . . . [which] would order the wheels through a jobber for the Budd Co., the motor from Continental Motors, the transmission from Borg-Warner, the seats and upholstery from Fisher Body . . . and it would all be assembled on the asphalt beside the gas pumps." [17]

LOCAL BUILDING CODES AS OBSTACLE TO INNOVATION

One reason—perhaps the principal one—for the absence of mass-produced housing is that there are 8,300 different local building codes in this country. They are, in the words of the Douglas commission, "thousands of little kingdoms, each having its own way"—"What goes in one town won't in another—and for no good reason." [18] President Johnson had specifically instructed the commission, Jan. 12, 1967, to "conduct a penetrating study of zoning, housing and building codes, taxation and development standards." He said: "These processes have not kept pace with the times. . . . They are the springboards from which many of the ills of urban life flow."

A commission staff analysis of 19 counties and six cities in Georgia, Maryland, North Carolina, Ohio and Virginia found 75 code requirements in excess of F.H.A. standards, each adding from $50 to $520 to the cost of what otherwise would be a $12,000 house. If a single manufacturer attempted to produce a standard product to meet all the code require-

---

[17] Walter McQuade, "An Assembly-Line Answer to the Housing Crisis," *Fortune*, May 1969, p. 99.

[18] National Commission on Urban Problems, *Building the American City* (1968), p. 21.

ments of that relatively small marketing area, the price of a $12,000 house would be increased by $2,492.

"Model" building codes have been devised and promoted by several major groups.[19] Most of them have accepted new cost-saving products and techniques for housing, such as plastic pipes for plumbing. But a major complaint is that codes at the local level, even when based on a model code, do not keep abreast of changes and soon become outdated. Few local governments have the resources to keep up with changes in technology or the stamina to oppose local interests that cling to the status quo.

"The problems faced by producers, builders, and professional people in the building industry, show unmistakably that alarms sounded over the past years about the building code situation have been justified," the Douglas commission concluded. "If anything, the case has been understated." A congressional mandate for the study had been included in the Housing and Urban Development Act of 1965. Congress asked, among other things, for recommendations on "what methods might be adopted to promote more uniform building codes." The commission recommended that a National Institute of Building Sciences be set up to issue uniform standards based on the most advanced technical criteria. It further recommended that Congress grant federal public-facility funds only to localities that had adopted those uniform standards.

ZONING ORDINANCES AND GROWTH OF MOBILE HOMES

While building codes inhibit innovation at on-site housing, local zoning ordinances restrict mobile homes—which accounted for 90 per cent of all housing sold under $15,000 in 1968 and for 25 per cent of all single-family homes. Selling for an average of only about $6,000, some 317,000 mobile homes went on the market in 1968, twice as many as five years earlier. Analysts are forecasting up to 400,000 sales in 1969. "Mobile home builders have moved in and filled the low-income housing vacuum," the *Wall Street Journal* commented July 8, 1968.

A large number of communities exclude mobile homes, either explicitly or by imposing zoning requirements which

---

[19] Among the most prominent are the Building Officials' Conference of America, the International Conference of Building Officials, the Southern Standard Building Code, and the National Building Code. In addition, there are mechanical codes, of which the two best known are the National Electrical Code and the National Plumbing Code.

manufacturers of mobile homes clearly cannot meet. These exclusionary practices reflect the view of residents who look upon mobile homes as unattractive "house trailers" and their occupants as nomadic people. "Mobile" may be a misnomer, because the Mobile Home Manufacturers Association reports that the average stay at one location is about five years.

Five million Americans now live in mobile homes, 80 per cent of them in mobile-home "parks" or "camps." These are usually found just beyond the city limits, and they range in quality from those providing spacious well-tended lots, golf courses and swimming pools to those in a cramped area behind a gas station and lacking even such amenities as electrical and plumbing outlets.

F.H.A. in May 1969 eased its rules on guaranteeing loans to developers of mobile-home sites. The agency said that henceforth it would insure up to 90 per cent of the loans on a 40-year basis, whereas past guarantees were limited to 75 per cent and 15 years. F.H.A. officials told Editorial Research Reports they expected also to ease their requirements for mobile-home buyers. A borrower may now be considered for F.H.A. financing if he removes the wheels and places the mobile-home unit on a permanent foundation on land that he owns. But in practice few such loans are made because the mobile home usually falls short of F.H.A. standards for single-family housing. Secretary Romney has indicated that he considers the techniques of mobile-home manufacturing the key to cheaper housing.

POSSIBILITIES IN NEW APPROACH TO HOUSE BUILDING

The Fruehauf Corporation, a builder of truck trailers and cargo containers, announced May 2, 1969, that it would begin manufacturing a three-bedroom house to retail for about $12,000. The outside walls will be made of aluminum and one room will be fitted against or atop the other as the owner desires. They will be placed on a prepared site and, unlike mobile homes, remain there.

A similar idea was on view to visitors at the Expo 67 world's fair in Montreal, where Israeli architect Moshe Safdie displayed Habitat, a bank of apartments cast as concrete boxes on the ground and lifted into place on a structural rack like gigantic shoe boxes. The drawback was that each four-bedroom unit of Habitat cost $150,000 to produce, about eight times the maximum for subsidized housing of the same size in New York. However, at the San Antonio HemisFair in 1968, the 496-room Hilton Palaccio del Rio hotel was constructed in a similar arrangement of concrete blocks at costs which the builder said were 20-25 per cent lower than by conventional methods. Construction required only 51 days.

This represents a step beyond mere prefabrication and is being called "systems building" or "systems technology." The words describe the process of bringing together materials and prefabricated parts on an assembly line and combining them into large and sometimes complex building elements. For 25 years or more, systems technology has been used by the Russians, French, Scandinavians and British, but in the United States it has rarely been removed from the drawing board.

The Douglas commission reported that the "systems" approach was reducing the cost of apartment building by 8 to 17 per cent in Europe. The commission surmised that savings of up to 25 per cent would be possible in the United States because American labor costs are higher than in Europe. "The most obvious housing application is in the construction of tall apartment buildings, with their vertical repetition, floor by floor, of identical elements," McQuade wrote. "But the repetition can occur in row houses, in developments of detached houses, in garden apartments, in any kind of large building development whose designer is ingenious enough to standardize the components to fit a production line." [20] He reported that the seven biggest private systems-building companies in Western Europe were negotiating affiliations with American companies to carry on their work in the United States. The Defense Department recently requested a systems approach to the experimental construction of a set of houses and barracks at George Air Force Base, Calif.

OPPOSITION OF CRAFT UNIONS; NEW LABOR PROPOSAL

About four million American construction workers are employed in 20 separate crafts, and each craft is represented by a separate labor union. They share the blame for some of the building industry's more regressive attitudes and practices. Yet organized labor is not of one mind. Walter P. Reuther, president of the United Automobile Workers, and a group of Detroit businessmen sponsored a contest among builders for designing and building low-cost housing. The

---

[20] Walter McQuade, *op. cit.*, p. 100.

winner, Prebuilt Homes, Inc., received a contract to furnish 800 factory-built houses. The plumbers union, however, balked at hooking up the plumbing when the concept was being tested.

Soon afterward, Reuther became the guiding force behind a plan announced June 3, 1969, by the Detroit Building Trades Council, to negotiate labor contracts with producers of factory-built housing in the area. The council called the plan "history-making" because workers would receive factory wages, rather than the higher rates received by members of building trades unions. The council, which itself is composed of AFL-CIO unions and four Teamsters locals, will attempt to organize the various workers, such as plumbers and carpenters and electricians, in an industrial rather than a craft union, as the U.A.W. organizes the different types of workers in the automobile industry.

Some unions have a tradition of promoting low-cost housing for workers. The Amalgamated Clothing Workers union was a pioneer 40 years or more ago in building cooperative apartment houses for workers in New York City. A number of similar projects, planned or financed by unions, followed. Cooperative apartment houses for middle and upper-income families also were introduced in the 1920s in New York and other cities.

New York City had some 57,000 units of cooperative housing in 1968, and 18,000 such units were under construction there—nearly all of the latter in Co-op City, a $400 million project intended to house 55,000 people in a series of towering apartments on a 300-acre site in the Bronx. Residents of cooperative housing purchase shares in the owning corporation and are thereby entitled to lease an apartment. Monthly maintenance charges are usually so much lower than the rental for comparable accommodations in commercial apartment houses that the occupant stands to gain even when allowance is made for loss of the income from the capital invested in the cooperative.

NEED OF FRESH INITIATIVE TO GET ADEQUATE HOUSING

All presidential commissions that have studied housing needs—the Douglas and Kaiser commissions, the Advisory Commission on Rural Poverty, the National Commission on Civil Disorders—agree on one point: Government initiative is needed to break the impasse that is depriving millions of adequate housing.

The Housing and Urban Development Act of 1968 has been characterized as the "most far-reaching housing legislation ever passed by Congress." [21] It set forth housing goals and extended home-buying assistance to families in the $3,000 to $6,500 income brackets. They were made eligible for a subsidy that would be the difference between 20 per cent of a family's monthly income and the mortgage payment. However, those earning less than $3,000, the official poverty line for an urban family of four, were untouched. The new housing programs do not envision replacement of public housing. In fact, HUD's goal this year is to double the production of public housing to 75,000 units. It plans to increase the number to 200,000 in 1972 and then taper off. Not even 100,000 units of public housing have been produced in any single year up to now.

Anthony Downs, a leading consultant on housing problems, has noted that to fulfill the housing goals set by Congress in 1968 would require total housing output to almost double, and production of moderate- and low-income housing to increase tenfold. Theoretically, all this could be achieved, he said, but only if throughout the 1970s there is (1) a great expansion of private capital for construction, (2) a big increase of building labor, (3) more subsidies for poor households, (4) suburban willingness to accept the city's poor, especially blacks, as neighbors, (5) technological advances in house building, and (6) strong efforts to remove official obstacles to those advances.

The first requirement (expansion of private construction capital) "would be virtually impossible unless we ended the war in Viet Nam immediately, avoided any costly new foreign involvements, placed top national priority on housing and adopted monetary and fiscal policies that encouraged low interest and relatively little inflation"; the second requirement (additional building labor) "involves major changes in existing union practices in the building trades"; and the third and fourth requirements would necessitate "a major change of attitude among middle-class Americans." [22] Downs

---

[21] See *1968 Congressional Quarterly Almanac*, pp. 313-335.

[22] Anthony Downs, "Moving Toward Realistic Housing Goals," *Agenda for the Nation* (Brookings Institution, 1968), pp. 151-153.

came to the "inescapable conclusion" that the goals will go unmet.

On an equally pessimistic note, the *American Builder,* in its centennial issue of November 1968, asked in bold headlines: "Who Really Gives a Damn About Housing?" The magazine answered its own question with smaller headlines, which read: "Not the Cities—They're headed for a decade of failure; Not the Suburbs—They couldn't care less; Not the rural areas—Everyone's leaving them; Not the power structure—All they do is talk, talk, talk."

Other analysts, while acknowledging the problems ahead, gain some satisfaction from the efforts of Americans to house themselves in the years after World War II. With millions of returning servicemen newly married and looking for a place to live, the nation faced a housing shortage at least as severe as the one now looming. A house-building boom got started and, despite a lot of catching up, housing needs actually decreased during the 1950s. According to an analysis made for the Douglas commission, the decade began with a need for 20.5 million new or rebuilt housing units and ended with a need for 15.4 million. Even with continued population growth and recent slippage in housing construction, the present decade will bring the nation's shortage of adequate housing down to about 10 million units. By that reckoning, it is in far better position today than it was 20 years ago.

But in that time, American expectations have risen in matters of housing as in other areas of life. A "decent home" and a "suitable environment" mean something different today than they did when first mentioned by Congress 20 years ago. For a great many people the words mean owning a single-family detached home in a neighborhood of one's choice. The black man has often found this aspiration unattainable because of racial prejudices; the middle-class white man is being frustrated in the same ambition because of economics—he can scarcely afford to be a home buyer.

Electric Power Problems

by

James G. Phillips

1 9 6 9
Dec. 17

ELECTRIC POWER PROBLEMS

A GROWING SHORTAGE of electric power is bewilder-
ing the American consumer. Blackouts and periods of
restricted power use have been experienced in virtually every
part of the country; no longer can a housewife assume she
will get current at the mere flick of a switch. Service by
electric utilities, generally speaking, has deteriorated because expansion of generating capacity has lagged far
behind an unprecedented surge of customer demand.[1]

Four years after the massive Northeast power blackout of
November 1965, large private power companies across the
country still have not installed the strong interconnections
between systems that the Federal Power Commission deems
necessary to ensure reliable service. And, in a battle that
dates back to the 1920s and 1930s, big private utilities continue to oppose expansion of public power projects. To com-
pound the problem, a number of badly needed new electric
generating plants have been held back by construction delays or by public concern lest they damage the environment.
Former F.P.C. Chairman Lee C. White has asserted that if
obstacles to expansion are not soon removed, rationing of
electricity—on either a voluntary or a mandatory basis—
may be inevitable.[2]

The national surge in demand for electric power is related
both to rapid population growth and to the successful efforts
of utilities and appliance manufacturers to promote new
uses of electricity. Annual sales of window air conditioners
have increased from 2.75 million to almost 5 million, and of
central air conditioning units for homes and office buildings

---

[1] The Federal Power Commission estimates that to meet demands for electric power
in periods of peak consumption will require total generating capacity of no less than
397.7 million kilowatts in 1975, 556.2 million kilowatts in 1980, and 1.1 billion kilowatts in 1990. Present installed capacity amounts to around 312 million kilowatts. A
kilowatt is a unit of power equal to 1,000 watts, and a kilowatt-hour is a unit of
energy equal to that expended by one kilowatt in one hour. A 100-watt electric light
bulb uses one kilowatt-hour of energy in 10 hours.

[2] Quoted in "Why Utilities Can't Meet Demand," *Business Week*, Nov. 29, 1969, p. 49.

from 700,000 to about 1.5 million, since 1964.[3] Sales of dishwashers, garbage disposal units, freezers and other heavy appliances likewise are booming. Although rates for electricity were almost halved between 1942 and 1967, the average annual household electric bill almost tripled during that period.

Utilities are producing 75 per cent more electricity now than they did in 1960, but electric power reserves have dwindled from about 30 per cent of capacity in 1960 to 16 per cent today—well below the 20 per cent reserve level considered adequate by the F.P.C. It has been estimated that even if utilities are able to follow through on present plans to add 148 million kilowatts of new capacity by 1974, the reserve percentage will remain virtually stationary.[4] The industry has been adding new customers at the rate of 2 per cent a year, while average annual consumption per customer has been increasing by 5 per cent. The prospects are for not only deteriorating service but also higher electric rates. To finance expansion plans, electric utilities as of Sept. 30, 1969, were asking state regulatory commissions for rate increases totaling more than $500 million.

CONTINUING THREAT OF SERIOUS POWER FAILURES

Since the big Northeast blackout on Nov. 9, 1965, there have been 37 major cascading power failures and numerous local power disruptions, in addition to "brownouts" in which customers are asked to restrict their use of electricity. In 1969, major power disruptions occurred in Miami, Fla., Providence, R. I., and Lansing, Mich., and less serious outages were reported from numerous other cities. On Sept. 3, a power failure halted trading on the New York Stock Exchange for half an hour, and on three other occasions New Yorkers were asked to refrain from using air conditioners and other heavy appliances. On July 18, the power "brownout" extended along the Eastern Seaboard from New York City to Washington, D. C.

After an 18-month study of the 1965 Northeast disturbance, the F.P.C. in July 1967 issued a three-volume report on *Prevention of Power Failures*. The report called on the major electric power companies to build additional high-

---

[3] Summertime peak demands have increased to such levels that at least one utility, the Virginia Electric and Power Co., has proposed a special summer rate surcharge to reimburse the company for costs of extra generating capacity.

[4] "Not Enough Electric Power—What to Do About It," *U.S. News & World Report*, Sept. 22, 1969, p. 86.

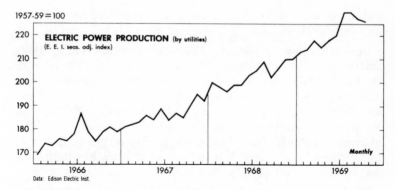

1957-59 = 100

220 — **ELECTRIC POWER PRODUCTION** (by utilities)
(E. E. I. seas. adj. index)

210

200

190

180

170 — Monthly

1966   1967   1968   1969

Data: Edison Electric Inst.

powered transmission links between systems to strengthen regional power networks against the threat of further cascading failures. The commission contended that the 1965 crisis could have been averted if connections between systems had been stronger.[5] The report also emphasized that companies on the interconnected systems could avoid local outages by borrowing power from other companies, and that interconnected companies could share power to meet individual peaking needs, thus saving large sums of money on unnecessary duplication of equipment. However, because of the high costs of installing additional transmission lines and a fear of increased federal regulation, the large utilities with the wherewithal to build the transmission lines have tended to resist the F.P.C.'s recommendations.[6]

Only one major recommendation out of a total of 34 specific F.P.C. proposals—the installation of load-shedding devices to cut off customers on an overheated line—has been widely accepted by the industry. One of the most persistent of the industry's critics, John Wicklein, a former *New York Times* reporter who now produces public affairs programs for the National Educational Television network, has asserted that load shedding "at best . . . can be only half—the negative half—of a program to protect against widespread blackouts." He says that "It is no substitute for adequate generating capacity and backup interconnections, but it does

---

[5] F.P.C. investigators found that the immediate cause of the 1965 blackout was the tripping-out of an overloaded transmission line from a hydroelectric plant on the Canadian side of the Niagara River. Cascading resulted because that area's transmission network was too weak to withstand the massive power surge that followed. The blackout left 30 million persons in a 30,000-square-mile area without electricity for periods of up to 13 hours. See "Electric Power Supply and Regulation," *E.R.R.*, 1965 Vol. II, pp. 941-958.

[6] The F.P.C.'s major powers are limited under existing law to the licensing of private hydroelectric projects on navigable waters and regulation of the sale of electricity in interstate commerce.

make a power company feel more secure politically to know its whole system won't go down at once." [7]

Concerned over industry inaction, Lee C. White, then chairman of the commission, asked Congress in 1968 to give the F.P.C. authority to order so-called reliability measures. Bills to increase the dependability of electric service have been introduced this year by individual members of Congress but have not emerged from committee. The present F.P.C. chairman, John N. Nassikas, a former New Hampshire utility lawyer who replaced White in August 1969, has indicated that he favors voluntary action by the utilities.

The industry estimates that it will spend $5 billion between 1969 and 1975 for new high-voltage interconnections. The F.P.C. contended when White was chairman that expenditure of $8 billion would be necessary to ensure acceptable levels of reliability. A commission study indicated that the annual cost of the additional $3 billion investment would be less than 2 per cent of the cost of supplying electric power to the whole country in 1975.[8]

ADVANTAGES OF EXTENDING POWER GRID SYSTEMS

At present, there are only three strong interconnected systems or "power grids" in the United States—a network built around the Tennessee Valley Authority area in the Southeast and another built around the Bonneville Power Administration project in the Pacific Northwest with interconnections along the length of the West Coast, and a private grid built by the American Electric Power Co. in Ohio and Indiana. There are no connections at all between power lines in Texas and lines in other states, because Texas utilities have sought to avoid regulation by the F.P.C. Links are particularly weak between Florida and other parts of the Southeast, between the Northwest and the northern mountain states, and between southeastern New York and the Pennsylvania-New Jersey-Maryland (PJM) network. Former F.P.C. Chairman White has called the New York-PJM interconnection "the single most important unbuilt power line in the U. S."

Some critics of the industry fear that additional major grids will not be developed short of another multi-state

---

[7] John Wicklein, "Where Will You Be When the Lights Go Out—Again?", *Washington Monthly,* September 1969, p. 16.

[8] Federal Power Commission, *Prevention of Power Failures, A Report to the President* (July 1967), Vol. 1, pp. 2-3.

power blackout or the passage of legislation arming the F.P.C. with greater authority. John Wicklein has suggested that the typical power company looks on its area "as a fief in which it is sovereign." He asserts: "The lords of the power fiefs have been concerned chiefly with turning a profit from local distribution of electricity. . . . If they were to interconnect with all the other companies, soon those other companies might start pressing to merge them into a single operating entity. And what lord wants to be merged out of his fief?" [9]

The standard of reliability sought by F.P.C. is the achievement of enough interconnected capacity so that any two major failures occurring simultaneously on any one system will not disrupt service throughout that system. The value of such a standard was demonstrated in 1969 on two of the three major interconnected networks. By borrowing power from other sources on the grids, power failures were averted when the two biggest generators on the American Electric Power network went out and when the main north-south interconnection tripped out on the Pacific Coast system.

Despite the continuing occurrence of power failures, private utilities frequently emphasize that the record they have achieved is 99.98 per cent perfect and that further improvement would be difficult to attain. *Electric World,* one of the industry's leading trade publications, boasted Oct. 27, 1969, that "Electric service reliability in this country is the envy of the rest of the world." It said interruptions for all American users averaged only 1¾ hours a year, compared with six hours in France and 17.5 hours in Great Britain. W. Donham Crawford, managing director of the Edison Electric Institute, the industry's major trade association, has said the few failures now occurring are due largely to uncontrollable events in local areas, such as wind storms, cars striking utility poles, etc.

The private electric companies have voluntarily formed 11 regional councils to work out reliability measures. The councils have made little demonstrable progress, however, and there have been reports that some of them recently barred F.P.C. engineers and representatives of municipal systems from their planning sessions. Proponents of grid

---

[9] John Wicklein, *op. cit.,* p. 12.

systems contend that exclusion of municipal systems would defeat the whole purpose of coordination, which requires that all systems in a region be tied together in a single interlocking grid.

CONSERVATIONIST OPPOSITION TO POWER PROJECTS

Growing national regard for environmental values has clashed increasingly with plans for utility expansion. Virtually every type of generating plant has come under attack —fossil-fuel (coal and oil) plants because they pollute the atmosphere and release thermal (heat) pollution into waters; nuclear plants because of thermal pollution and radiation hazards; and hydroelectric projects because of contentions that they mar the landscape of otherwise scenic rivers. Some industry officials describe the conservationist opposition as the biggest of all their hurdles.

Perhaps the most heated of the conservationist battles has come in New York City, where the Consolidated Edison Co. has encountered opposition to almost every new generating plant it has proposed. A particularly strong clamor was raised by Con Ed's plan to build a huge hydroelectric project at Storm King Mountain on the Hudson River, 40 miles from New York City. Delay over the project, which has been tied up at the F.P.C. and in the courts for more than six years, has made it necessary for the company to retain a number of uneconomical coal-fired steam plants that it had hoped to phase out years ago. Con Ed President Charles F. Luce has said that if the opposition continues, "eventually it will have an effect when you try to switch on the light." [10]

An important licensing concept for nuclear generating plants is at stake in Minneapolis, where the Minnesota Pollution Control Agency has denied a permit for a nuclear plant approved by the U. S. Atomic Energy Commission. The state agency, which contends that the A.E.C. rules on radio emissions are not stringent enough, has written its own set of regulations. The Northern States Power Co., which already has completed the plant, contends that the state regulations are too harsh and has challenged them in state and federal courts.

Conservationist opposition to new generating facilities has emerged in a number of other areas. Among projects

---

[10] Jeremy Main, "A Peak Load of Troubles for the Utilities," *Fortune*, November 1969, pp. 200, 205.

under dispute are a proposed nuclear plant at Calvert Cliffs overlooking the Chesapeake Bay in Maryland, a proposed high-tension transmission line that would pass close to the Civil War battlefield of Antietam at Sharpsburg, Md., a hydroelectric project at Sunfish Pond near the Delaware Water Gap in New Jersey, and proposed nuclear plants in Vermont and elsewhere.

At least two government officials have indicated sympathy with the industry's position. In testimony before the Joint Congressional Atomic Energy Committee on Oct. 29, 1969, A.E.C. Chairman Glenn T. Seaborg charged that some conservationists were engaging in "unsubstantiated fear-mongering" and "hysteria" in opposing the nuclear plants. Should the critics prevail, he said, "in the years ahead, today's outcries about the environment will be nothing compared to cries of angry citizens who find that power failures due to a lack of sufficient generating capacity to meet peak loads have plunged them into prolonged blackouts—not mere minutes of inconvenience, but hours, perhaps days— when their health and well-being, and that of their families, may be seriously endangered." With "good planning and work," Seaborg added, "we can have safe, clean and reliable nuclear power, as much of it as we need." F.P.C. Chairman Nassikas has asserted that in jurisdictional disputes such as the Minnesota controversy A.E.C. rules should take precedence.

Conservationists have indicated an intention to step up efforts to prevent construction of plants which they think will damage the environment. Michael McCloskey, conservation director of the Sierra Club, has said: "Our strategy is going to be to sue and sue and sue. Eventually, the utilities are going to have to take us seriously and decide there has to be a better way to arrive at decisions." The hand of the conservationists was strengthened recently by a federal appeals court ruling in New York that it was unnecessary for conservationists to prove a direct financial interest in a project to be permitted to intervene in hearings before regulatory bodies. It was sufficient, the court ruled, that such a group represent the public interest.

Development and Regulation of Utilities

FROM THE DAY Thomas Alva Edison invented the electric light bulb in 1879, growth of the nation's electric power has been phenomenal. By 1880, the first water-wheel-driven electric generator for arc lights was installed in Rochester, N.Y. In 1882, Edison opened his famed Pearl Street generating plant in downtown New York City—the world's first steam electric generator. By 1902, there were 2,805 central generating plants serving most of the urban areas of the country. Over every decade since 1880, the country's use of electricity has doubled.

In the early days of the industry, the area which electric light companies could supply was sharply limited by the short distances over which the direct current then in use could be distributed. Many cities in the 1880s were served by a number of different generating systems, some of them serving only a few homes or stores, even a single office building. The situation changed radically with development in 1886 of the alternating current transformer, which made it possible for a central distribution network to serve much larger areas through use of higher-voltage transmission and distribution facilities. Transmission-line voltages rose from a maximum of 3 kilovolts in 1886 to 60 kilovolts in 1901, and a comparable increase took place in the size of individual generating units.[11]

By the turn of the century, many of the smaller utilities found it economical to merge with larger ones and to extend greatly their service areas. Soon, the typical pattern of utility operation took the form of monopoly, making it necessary for states and municipalities to set up licensing procedures and regulatory bodies.

Over the years, three different types of utilities developed—private investor-owned companies, publicly owned local systems (municipals), and privately owned rural cooperatives. In mid-1969, there were about 500 investor-owned companies serving 79 per cent of the country's electricity users, about 2,000 municipals serving 13.5 per cent, and 1,100 rural cooperatives serving the remaining 7.5 per cent. The investor-owned companies produced about 76 per

[11] Federal Power Commission, *National Power Survey* (October 1964), Vol. I, p. 14.

cent of the total power supply, the federal government (which sells power wholesale to all three types of utilities) 13 per cent, locally owned public systems 10 per cent, and the rural co-ops 1 per cent. The electric power industry has become the nation's biggest business, with capital assets 60 per cent greater than those of the next largest industry— petroleum refining. The United States, with 6 per cent of world population, now accounts for 36 per cent of global electric power.

RIVALRY OF THE PRIVATE AND NON-PRIVATE UTILITIES

Inevitably, animosity developed between investor-owned companies on one hand and the municipals and co-ops on the other. The focal point of controversy was the entry of the government into power production, a development the municipals and co-ops supported and investor-owned companies opposed.

The controversy began taking shape during the 1920s, when private utilities were forming giant electric utility holding companies. The big holding companies were often able to pressure small municipal systems into selling out, and they were able also to exert considerable pressure on regulatory commissions to sanction high rate structures.[12] During the New Deal era of the 1930s, the government moved decisively to break up the holding companies and to establish power facilities of its own. Congress in 1935 passed the Public Utility Holding Company Act, which limited each company to a single interconnected system serving contiguous territories. Two years earlier, it had set up the Tennessee Valley Authority to conduct a multi-purpose river development program that included generation and marketing of electricity.

Congress in time established federal hydroelectric power projects in almost every section of the country. The Federal Power Act of 1935, which superseded the Federal Water Power Act of 1920, extended F.P.C. jurisdiction to interstate transmission of electricity and gave the commission authority to regulate rates for sale of such power at wholesale. Previously, F.P.C. had been concerned only with issuing licenses for non-federal hydroelectric projects.[13]

---

[12] Arthur M. Schlesinger Jr., *The Crisis of the Old Order* (1956), pp. 118-124.

[13] See "Power Policies of the Roosevelt Administration," *E.R.R.*, 1933 Vol. II, pp. 331-335.

Another aspect of the New Deal power program was the provision of financing for electrification of rural areas to which private utilities had found it unprofitable to extend service. Congress in 1936 set up the Rural Electrification Administration to offer low-cost loans to nonprofit cooperatives established to provide electric service. Interest on R.E.A. loans, fixed at 2 per cent in 1944, has remained at that figure despite repeated efforts by the investor-owned utilities to persuade Congress to increase the rate.

Generally speaking, it was not the intention of the Roosevelt administration to create an all-public nonprofit power system to serve the whole country. Its aim was to bring about enough competition to force the private utilities to lower their rates and extend and improve their services. Thus the main purpose of the federal power program was to establish a "yardstick" against which to measure the performance of the private power industry. An additional objective was to make certain that municipal systems and co-ops had access to low-cost and dependable sources of power.[14]

Every year since 1946, when the F.P.C. began to publish statistics of the electric power companies, rates charged by public power systems have been substantially lower than those charged by private utilities. In 1967, the last full year for which statistics are available, private utility rates averaged 2.31¢ per kilowatt-hour as against an average of 1.49¢ for public power systems. Nonetheless, advocates of public power argue that the private companies' rates would be far higher without the "yardstick" competition of public power. Private utilities contend that the municipals and co-ops enjoy an unfair advantage in not having to pay corporation income taxes, and that the low-cost government loans give the co-ops an additional advantage over investor-owned utilities.

Private utilities remain strongly opposed to public power —a position some observers consider unreasonable at a time when the nation is threatened by a power shortage. The

[14] The New Deal power projects, as well as a few earlier federal power projects, gave public agencies (such as federal installations, municipally owned systems, and similar state, district and county marketing groups) and nonprofit rural electric cooperatives a prior right, ahead of private utilities, to purchase federally produced power. This "public power preference" was made general and permanent by the Reclamation Project Act of 1939 and the Flood Control Act of 1944. See Congressional Quarterly's *Congress and the Nation*, Vol. I, 1965, p. 774.

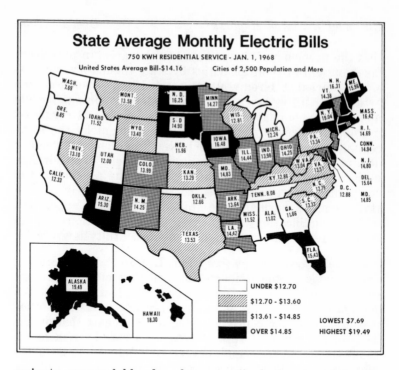

State Average Monthly Electric Bills

750 KWH RESIDENTIAL SERVICE - JAN. 1, 1968

United States Average Bill-$14.16   Cities of 2,500 Population and More

UNDER $12.70	
$12.70 - $13.60	
$13.61 - $14.85	LOWEST $7.69
OVER $14.85	HIGHEST $19.49

private power lobby has been particularly strong in the Northeast, where electric rates are the highest in the country and there is no major federal "yardstick" project. Although Congress in 1965 authorized a $300 million federal project—the Dickey-Lincoln School Dams on the St. John River in Maine—vigorous lobbying by private New England utilities resulted in denial of appropriations for the project. The companies opposing Dickey-Lincoln developed an "over-all strategy" paper which stated the following objectives: "To develop a regional climate of public opinion which will prevent any expansion of government-owned or tax-subsidized electricity within New England, and which will, instead, permit the gradual elimination of government power operations presently existing in the area."

ATTACKS ON THE STATE REGULATORY COMMISSIONS

As an alternative to Dickey-Lincoln, the New England utilities have proposed building a private nuclear plant of their own, Maine Yankee, which they contend would bring power to the region at less cost than Dickey-Lincoln. As in other private projects in the New England area, the utilities have sought to exclude municipal systems from participation.

Some critics of the electric utility industry have contended

93

that the problems of the private utilities arise in part from lax oversight of their activities by state regulatory commissions. Journalist Jeremy Main asserted in a recent *Fortune* article: "Utility executives are generally unimaginative men, grown complacent on private monopoly and regulated profits. Nor are they spurred to improvement by the state regulatory commissions, which seem neither willing nor able to prod the utilities into action." [15] John Wicklein has declared that state commissions "are in the pockets of the companies they are supposed to regulate." He says: "The state agencies normally are staffed by political appointees with no qualifications for judging utility operations and no stomach for challenging highly qualified utility lawyers." [16]

In their book *Overcharge,* Sen. Lee Metcalf (D Mont.) and his aide Victor Reinemer argued that most regulatory commissions were understaffed and thus had to accept the contentions of utilities as to their revenue needs and other matters. Metcalf recently asserted in the Senate that on the basis of a 6 per cent rate of return on rate base, a figure widely accepted by regulatory commissions as reasonable, the country's utilities overcharged consumers by $1.4 billion in 1967 alone.[17]

Because utilities are allowed to treat such items as charitable donations, lobbying and advertising expenditures, and the cost of preparing rate cases as operating expenses, Metcalf and other critics contend that the rates allowed have actually resulted in even greater overcharges. Private utilities insist that these expenditures constitute a justifiable cost of doing business.

Armed with data from his book, Metcalf carried his attack on state regulatory commissions to Congress. He and 11 other senators sponsored a bill to set up an independent Office of Utility Consumers' Counsel which would represent consumers in rate proceedings before federal and state agencies that regulate electric, gas and telephone companies. The bill also would establish a grant program to promote study of regulatory matters, and it would authorize the

---

[15] Jeremy Main, *op. cit.,* p. 118.

[16] John Wicklein, *op. cit.,* p. 20.

[17] Regulatory commissions allow utilities to set rates for electric service high enough to cover operating expenses plus a fixed percentage return on their investment in plant and equipment—their rate base. The base includes both paid-in capital and earnings reinvested in capital goods. Some commissions have allowed returns far in excess of the generally accepted standard of 6 per cent.

F.P.C. to require utilities to report uniformly on the make-up of their rate bases and other operating criteria.

In introducing the bill, Jan. 24, 1969, Metcalf said utility regulation was "mythical" and that the "myth" was "perpetuated by the industries themselves, at the customer's expense, through their advertising and public relations programs." He went on to say: "When regulation is actually attempted, the utilities' research, presentations and consultants are financed from customer-paid operating expenses. . . . However, no provision is made, through either the tax or rate structure, for similar presentation of the public case. The utilities do not want that, and their view prevails."

At hearings before the Senate Government Operations Subcommittee on Intergovernmental Relations, the Metcalf bill drew stiff opposition from private electric utilities and the National Association of Regulatory Utility Commissioners. Edwin Vennard, representing the Edison Electric Institute, told the subcommittee on April 22, 1969, that consumers were already "adequately represented" and that the measure would only "confuse the regulatory process" and "mislead rather than help consumers."

Under present regulatory practices, Vennard pointed out, there had been a very substantial decrease in electric rates since the end of World War II in contrast to a large increase of prices in general. George I. Bloom, representing the regulatory commissioners, testified that the proposed consumers' counsel "could not do more for consumers than most of the commissions now do for them." Strong support for the measure has nevertheless developed among consumer groups and some state regulatory commissions and individual commissioners; a Senate showdown is expected early in 1970.

Nuclear Power and Financing Problems

PROSPECTS for a low-cost buildup of the nation's electric power supplies appear to hinge on the performance of nuclear steam-generating plants, a new technology that has gained wide acceptance among the larger electric utilities. The Atomic Energy Commission has estimated that the nation's nuclear generating capacity will build up swiftly from 3.9 million kilowatts in 1969 to 150 million kilowatts by 1980, when it will reach 25 per cent of total capacity. By the year 2000, the A.E.C. estimates that 50 per cent of capacity and virtually all orders for new generators will be nuclear. As of Sept. 30, 1969, 15 nuclear plants were in operation, 48 under construction, and 41 more under design.

Despite the high costs of nuclear plants, proponents of nuclear power contend they will save substantial sums of money because of the economies of scale they expect to attain through larger generating capacities. In the early 1960s, a coal-fired generating plant with a capacity of 100,000 kilowatts was considered a large plant. Although coal-fired plants of 600,000 to 700,000 kilowatts are now under development, most of the new nuclear plants have capacities in excess of one million kilowatts, and plants with capacities of up to four million kilowatts are being developed. Other arguments put forward by the nuclear power advocates are that nuclear plants cause far less air pollution than fossil-fuel plants, that they usually are more pleasing to the eye, and that additional economies will result in areas where fossil fuels must be hauled in from long distances.

The A.E.C. has emphasized that even bigger economies of scale can be realized when fast-breeder reactors, which produce more fuel than they consume, come into operation in the early 1980s. A.E.C. Chairman Seaborg told the Edison Electric Institute, June 9, 1969, that within 30 years after the breeders are introduced, "nuclear-power generating systems could become self-sustaining . . . providing fuel for new reactors as needed and with such efficient use of nuclear fuel that our supplies are sufficient to last hundreds or even thousands of years." Seaborg cited an A.E.C. study which estimated that over the period 1970-2020, which would include the development cycle of fast breeders, they would save a grand total of $9.1 billion (in 1970 dollars) over a power economy based on a mix of coal-fired and present nuclear reactors.

CURRENT DELAYS IN NUCLEAR POWER DEVELOPMENT

Cost benefits of nuclear generators have still to be demonstrated. A study cited in the trade magazine *Nuclear Industry* found that costs of new nuclear and fossil-fuel plants completed in 1969 averaged $127 per kilowatt for coal plants and $159 for nuclear. The study estimated that by 1975 the gap would widen slightly to $186 for coal and

$228 for nuclear. Jack K. Horton, chairman and chief executive officer of the Southern California Edison Co., has said that construction delays for nuclear power projects would cost electric utilities at least $425 million over the next four years, including carrying charges and cost escalation for equipment and labor. Construction of nuclear plants is said to be running six months to two years behind schedule.

The delays result in part from unexpected construction problems and public opposition and in part from an industry misforecast of future power needs, which led to a crush of demand for new plants when the higher demand levels were finally projected in the mid-1960s. John W. Simpson, president of the power systems division of the Westinghouse Electric Corp., has said that "The cyclical pattern of orders for new generating capacity and the underbuying of a few years ago is probably the major reason for the power shortages that exist in some utility systems today." Simpson noted that orders for nuclear generating capacity had fluctuated from about 17 million kilowatts in 1964 to 60 million in 1967, 30 million in 1968, and back to 60 million in 1969.

An even bigger problem for nuclear power advocates is to convince the public that the benefits from increased generating capacity will outweigh any harm to the environment. In testimony before the Joint Atomic Energy Committee on Nov. 4, 1969, Dr. Raymond E. Johnson, assistant director of the Interior Department's Bureau of Sport Fisheries and Wildlife, said that "few major interstate streams" had not been affected by heated discharges from either nuclear or conventional generators, and that "from the announced plans of the industry to increase its generation capacity, it appears that the future heat load on the aquatic environment will be stupendous." Johnson and other environmental experts told the committee that an increase in temperatures of only a few degrees could kill a variety of aquatic organisms.[18] The Federal Water Pollution Control Administration recently announced that a 15-degree increase in temperatures at a fossil-fuel plant on Biscayne Bay near Miami caused a "very extensive" kill of fish, and other aquatic life.

---

[18] In both nuclear and fossil-fuel plants, water is pumped in from streams to serve as a coolant to condense the steam that produces electricity. The environmental effect of waste heat is considered more severe in the case of nuclear plants because they will be far larger than conventional plants.

Some conservationists fear that the nuclear plants may emit unacceptable levels of radiation. Although waste material from the reactor is removed and buried, small amounts of radioactive substances escape through the reactor's smokestack and through seepage into its coolant. The A.E.C. has set restrictions on emissions, but some scientists question whether they are tight enough.[19]

The intensity of the clash between conservationists and power interests has made it increasingly likely that the government will be called on to develop some mechanism to bring such controversies to rapid settlement. Under present procedures, court cases or agency hearings may drag on for months or years while power needs go unfulfilled. F.P.C. Commissioner Carl E. Bagge thinks the best solution is to set up a committee of impartial experts to study and make recommendations on plant siting to the F.P.C. and local regulatory bodies. Either the commission or Congress should establish such a committee "at once," he said, "before the environmental crisis facing the utilities becomes intellectually unmanageable and irresponsive to reasonable public and private action."

PROPOSED LEGISLATION TO PROTECT ENVIRONMENT

Bills addressed to the environmental and reliability problems are currently pending in Congress. Companion bills by Sen. Edward M. Kennedy (D Mass.) and Rep. Richard L. Ottinger (D N.Y.) would create a National Council on the Environment, appointed by the President, which would have authority to pass on the environmental aspects of all proposals before the F.P.C. for generating facilities or transmission lines. The bills would empower the F.P.C. itself to approve or disapprove all plans for power-generating facilities in excess of 200,000 kilowatts, promulgate compulsory reliability regulations, and, in consultation with utilities, set up regional councils to work out comprehensive development plans to strengthen coordination of regional power systems through interconnections and other measures. The F.P.C. would be authorized to accept or reject the plans depending on whether they were consistent with the commission's criteria. A similar measure, introduced by Sen. Edmund S. Muskie (D Maine), would create regional power boards re-

---

[19] Sheldon Novick, "The Menace of the Peaceful Atom," *Commentary*, December 1968, pp. 33-39.

sponsible to federal agencies designated by the President. The agencies would develop standards for reliability and environmental protection to be enforced by the boards.

Current prospects for passage of any of the pending bills are considered dim. Ottinger said recently: "Judging from the character of this administration, I don't think we would get any support for a reliability bill. This administration is much more business-oriented than the last one and wouldn't be likely to push a bill that the industry opposed."

PROSPECTIVE EXPANSION COSTS AND RATE INCREASES

To keep up with the demand for electricity, the power industry must raise unprecedented amounts of capital, and it must do so in the face of rising public opposition to rate increases, growing competition from gas, and the highest borrowing costs in history.

Edwin Vennard, then managing director for the Edison Electric Institute, told the Senate Intergovernmental Relations Subcommittee on April 22, 1969, that utilities would have to increase spending on new equipment from the current level of $8 billion a year to $12 billion by 1980. Those figures compared with total spending of only about $3 billion annually, or a total of $74 billion, for the whole period since World War II. F.P.C. Chairman Nassikas has estimated that utilities will have to spend $300 billion to $350 billion by 1990, or an average of $14 billion to $17 billion a year. Utility executives expect about half of the expansion to be funded out of profits and the other half by borrowing.

The financing problem is complicated by the fact that low-interest bonds issued by the utilities for expansion after World War II are now coming due for repayment, forcing the industry to seek refinancing at interest rates almost three times the levels prevailing in the late 1940s. According to a study by the Chase-Manhattan Bank, the private utilities will have to refinance $600 million worth of bonds annually throughout the 1970s as compared with only $100 million a year in the 1960s.

In view of inflation and the new capital needs, utility executives are arguing that state regulatory commissions should allow returns of 7 to 8 per cent instead of the generally accepted (but often exceeded) norm of 6 per cent. Economist Leon H. Keyserling, chairman of the President's

Council of Economic Advisers under President Truman, told the Senate Intergovernmental Relations Subcommittee, April 22, 1969, that to ensure adequate investment growth, utilities should have been permitted to earn net operating incomes of $4.2 billion in 1968 against an actual figure of $3.7 billion. Keyserling predicted that if regulatory policies remained the same, utilities would fall $900 million short of annual capital needs by 1972 and $1.7 billion short by 1977. "These industries," Keyserling said, "have lived in recent years under a regulatory process which, in the misguided zeal to offer the consumer the lowest attainable rates in the short run, has deprived these industries of the funds and incentives required to invest enough in plant and equipment expansion, and in technological research and innovation, to optimize services to the consumer in the long run."

To finance their expansion, electric utilities have asked state regulatory commissions for rate increases totaling more than $500 million, according to figures compiled recently by Sen. Metcalf. Consolidated Edison of New York City, for example, is seeking a rate boost that would give it additional revenue amounting to $117.5 million; Commonwealth Edison of Chicago wants an additional $45 million; Virginia Electric and Power Co., which serves most of Virginia and parts of North Carolina and West Virginia, $25 million; and Duquesne Electric Co. of Pittsburgh, $19 million. Throughout the country, higher rates are being vigorously opposed by consumers, who consider it unconscionable for the industry to charge more at a time when its service is becoming less rather than more reliable.

Concern over reliability of New York City's electric supply system was voiced by the Federal Power Commission on Dec. 12, 1969, in a review of Consolidated Edison Co.'s 10-year plans. The F.P.C. review said: "Potential power shortages, similar to those that occurred a number of times this past summer, may possibly recur during the 1970 summer peak load season, and meeting demands in 1974 and 1977 could be problems." The F.P.C. said that Con Edison should undertake at once a canvass of all utilities in the Northeast and other service areas to acquire assistance in power emergencies. The race along the Eastern Seaboard, as well as elsewhere, is between galloping consumption of electricity and completion of new power plants.

FEDERAL BUDGET MAKING

by

Hoyt Gimlin

1 9 6 9
Jan. 8

FEDERAL BUDGET MAKING

F EDERAL budget making is the process of sorting out national priorities. The complex and painstaking exercise forces the White House to make hard choices involving competing constituencies and political pressures. By having to put a price tag on its goals, the administration must choose between what it considers attainable and what is merely desirable.

These choices are now being made by Richard M. Nixon and his advisers but, like all incoming Presidents in recent times, Nixon must live for a while with the budget he inherits from the departing incumbent. President Johnson will present to Congress on or about Jan. 13,[1] one week before he leaves office, the federal budget for the fiscal year 1970, beginning next July 1. Nixon is certain to revise it, but probably not entirely as he would like.

President Eisenhower in 1953 found little room to maneuver in the budget President Truman had left him for fiscal 1954. Eisenhower cut it by $4.5 billion but still felt impelled to ask Congress to postpone tax reductions which he wanted. President Kennedy in 1961 added $8 billion to the last Eisenhower budget but was unable to win from Congress that year a series of tax revisions to stimulate the economy.[2]

Eisenhower waited until May to deliver his first budget message to Congress, while Kennedy sent his up in March. A Nixon economic adviser, Herbert Stein, has suggested that the President-elect might follow the Eisenhower example. The delay would give Nixon more time to decide whether to ask Congress to retain the 10 per cent surtax on corporate and personal income. The tax was enacted for one year only and, unless renewed, will lapse on June 30, 1969.

---

[1] The President is required by law to send an annual budget to Congress within 15 days of the opening of each regular session.

[2] See "Fiscal and Budget Policy," *E.R.R.*, 1962 Vol. II, pp. 557-572, and *Congress and the Nation, 1945-1964* (1965), pp. 413, 427.

Two *Wall Street Journal* writers have described the surtax decision as "Mr. Nixon's central dilemma"—"Either he asks Congress to prolong President Johnson's unpopular surtax beyond its mid-1969 expiration date or puts his own stamp on a budget deficit bigger and potentially more inflationary than his Democratic predecessor ever dared to propose for a coming year." They added that the new President would face the same arithmetic in May as in February "unless the Viet Nam War is unquestionably settled by spring." [3]

PRESIDENT-ELECT NIXON AND THE INCOME SURTAX

Nixon said during the 1968 presidential campaign that he wished to let the surtax die, and Rep. Wilbur D. Mills (D Ark.), chairman of the tax-writing House Ways and Means Committee, has indicated that it will die unless Nixon pushes for its renewal. "It is utterly impossible for Congress to pass a tax increase or a continuance of a temporary increase," Mills said in a speech before the Tax Foundation in New York on Dec. 4, "without the full support, the very active support of the White House." Less than a month earlier, on Nov. 10, he had voiced doubt that the Democratic-controlled Congress would go along with Nixon's expressed desire to drop or reduce the surtax.

Maurice Stans, who will become Secretary of Commerce in the Nixon cabinet, told a news conference in Washington on Dec. 19 that he hoped the surcharge would be halved to 5 per cent on July 1 and eliminated entirely one year later. On the day Stans spoke, President Johnson forecast a "small" budget surplus—the first in nine years—when the fiscal year 1969 ends on June 30. The economy has expanded at a faster pace than was anticipated in January 1968, when an $8 billion deficit was projected for fiscal 1969. "I hope it will be possible to submit a budget in January which will continue the small surplus," Johnson said in his Dec. 19 statement. This was generally interpreted to mean that he would propose keeping expenditures under $200 billion and urge continuation of the surtax.

Washington Post reporter Frank Porter wrote the following day that the President's statement indicated that Nixon would "receive from his predecessor in January a fiscal blueprint of impeccable appeal to his own conservative constitu-

---

[3] Richard F. Janssen and John Pierson, *Wall Street Journal*, Nov. 14, 1968.

(in millions of dollars)

Fiscal year	Net receipts	Net expenditures	Surplus or deficit
1960	77,763	76,539	1,224
1961	77,659	81,515	—3,856
1962	81,409	87,787	—6,378
1963	86,376	92,642	—6,266
1964	89,459	97,684	—8,226
1965	93,072	96,507	—3,435
1966	104,727	106,978	—2,251
1967	115,794	125,732	—9,938
1968*	153,676	172,803	—25,187**

* Recalculated, Dec. 24, 1968, on basis of unified budget. Figures for previous years on basis of administrative budget.

** Difference between receipts and expenditures was $19,127 million. Above overall deficit includes deficit of $6,059 million in federal loan accounts.

ency." Porter pointed out that "If the President-elect, who will have the actual responsibility for implementing next year's budget, goes into the red, he will appear to be confounding his own precepts."

INFLATION AND THE METHODS USED TO COMBAT IT

Some economic analysts have suggested that even if the President-elect could see budgetary daylight without the surtax, he might have to retain it to avert runaway inflation. The cost-of-living index, as recorded by the Bureau of Labor Statistics, rose for the 22nd straight month in November. It reflected a price rise of 4.4 per cent in consumer products and services during the first 11 months of 1968, the highest since 1951 when, in the midst of the Korean War, the year-long increase climbed to 5.9 per cent. Because of the "big problem" of inflation, *The Magazine of Wall Street* commented, Nov. 23, that "the immediate course the 37th President will take has been largely preordained."

Paul W. McCracken, who will become chairman of the Council of Economic Advisers under Nixon, has said: "We ought to get the rate of inflation below 3 per cent—hopefully down in the 2 per cent zone by mid-1969." A lower rate, McCracken added, might cause unemployment to rise above "socially tolerable" levels.[4] To achieve a 2-3 per cent range, he asserted, "the budget deficit must be kept within the size limits where it can readily be financed in the credit market without drawing monetary policy off course."

Borrowing in recent years to finance budget deficits, and re-finance outstanding government issues, has occasionally

[4] Quoted by *U. S. News & World Report*, Nov. 25, 1968, p. 42.

put severe strain on the money markets. The government has competed with private enterprise for lendable money. It conducts its borrowing through sales of bonds and other securities. To find buyers, the government has been forced to offer record-high interest rates. Treasury bills due in 90 days, the bellwether items of the short-term money market, bore interest above 6 per cent for the first time in offerings made in late December 1968. Corporate bonds of the highest quality were then paying only a fraction below 7 per cent. Rates for bank lending climbed to 7½ per cent or more in the wake of Federal Reserve Board action on Dec. 17 raising the "discount rate" of Federal Reserve lending to member banks by a quarter of a percentage point—to 5½ per cent.

The Federal Reserve has responded to the unusual combination of inflation and high interest rates by alternately contracting the money supply, to choke off inflation, and expanding it when credit got exceedingly tight.[5] Nixon has been critical of these ups and downs, but he has held that the Federal Reserve Board had no other choice because the White House was reluctant for too long to reduce spending and raise taxes. Johnson requested a surtax in 1967, but Congress favored spending cuts instead. Finally, in June 1968, it imposed both a 10 per cent surtax and a spending ceiling of $180 billion for fiscal 1969. Congress later voted exemptions from the spending cuts amounting to $6 billion, and on Dec. 19 Johnson predicted that total spending would fall $1.6 billion below the revised ceiling of $186 billion.

McCracken said recently that "from mid-1965 to late 1967 the management of monetary policy was exceedingly poor" because it allowed a clearly inflationary expansion of the money supply.[6] McCracken's view had been elicited by the House Banking and Currency Subcommittee on Domestic Finance. The chairman of the subcommittee and of its parent committee is Rep. Wright Patman (D Texas), who has long been critical of Federal Reserve Board Chairman Wil-

---

[5] See "National Debt Management," *E.R.R.*, 1967 Vol. II, pp. 885-902.

[6] The money supply is expanded by purchases of government securities by the Federal Reserve System. Suppose the Fed buys $1 million of Treasury bills from a New York dealer in government securities. It pays for the securities with a check issued on itself. The dealer deposits the check in his account at a commercial bank. The bank sends it in for collection. Upon clearance, the commercial bank is credited with $1 million in its reserve account at a Federal Reserve bank. In this way the government "creates" money. Expansion of the money supply does not stop there, however, because a commercial bank can make loans aggregating more than six times the value of its reserves. By a reverse process, the Fed can shrink the money supply by selling government securities to dealers, who pay by checks drawn on commercial banks. The reserve accounts of commercial banks in the Federal Reserve System are thereby drawn down.

liam McChesney Martin's tight money policies. The sub-committee reported Dec. 29, 1968, that more than two-thirds of 71 economists responding to a questionnaire "favored making the growth of the money supply the target of monetary policy."

The results of the questionnaire indicated growing support for the "Chicago school" of economists led by Milton Friedman of the University of Chicago. They believe that the Federal Reserve should concentrate, not on interest rates, but on achieving a steady and moderate growth of the money supply. Arthur M. Okun, outgoing chairman of the Council of Economic Advisers, takes the opposite view. Interest rates and credit availability should be the Fed's main concern, he told the Patman subcommittee. "There is no simple and apparent relation between the money supply and the G.N.P. [Gross National Product]," Okun added.

In theory and often in practice, the Federal Reserve is independent of the Executive Branch as well as of Congress. Fiscal and monetary policies are often uncoordinated and sometimes work at cross purposes. Since Martin's economic conservatism is more attuned to Nixon's views than to Johnson's, it is expected that the relationship between the Federal Reserve and the White House will become closer. The Federal Reserve Board's action in raising the discount rate on Dec. 17 was viewed in some quarters as a tip-off that Nixon wanted to employ monetary as well as fiscal restraints to curb inflation.

ECONOMIC PHILOSOPHY OF NIXON'S KEY ADVISERS

The London *Economist* commented recently that there was "every reason to expect" the incoming Secretary of the Treasury, David M. Kennedy, "to regard the inflation problem as urgent and deadly serious and to use the orthodox weapon of a balanced or near-balanced budget to fight it." This would be the case, the magazine added, "even if Mr. Kennedy had fallen under the spell of the 'Chicago School' of monetary economists, who are arguing persuasively that only the money supply, not the budget deficit, matters."

> Middle-grounders, and these almost certainly include Mr. Kennedy, admit that the supply of money may be very important. But the Federal Reserve cannot in practice restrain its growth if the successful financing of a huge budgetary deficit has to be assured. So whichever school of economists is right, the answer in present circumstances comes out the same: a tough budget. . . .[7]

---

[7] "A Sledgehammer for Inflation?" *The Economist*, Dec. 21, 1968, p. 27.

The Secretary of the Treasury, the chairman of the Council of Economic Advisers, and the director of the Bureau of the Budget are sometimes known in Washington as the "troika" of economic policy planners. Nixon has indicated that Stans, as Secretary of Commerce, will join this inner group, making it a "quadriad"; Stans was budget director (1957-60) when Eisenhower was President. Kennedy has been board chairman of the Continental Illinois Bank & Trust Co., and McCracken, the council's new chairman, a professor of business administration at the University of Michigan. The new budget director is to be Robert Mayo, who has been a vice president of the same Chicago bank.

The Mayo appointment caused some surprise in Washington because Kennedy was his superior at the bank. The question asked was whether the same relationship would continue into government. But Edwin L. Dale reported in the *New York Times* on Dec. 15 that Mayo had already given assurance that "I will be the President's man, not the Treasury's man." Dale quoted an unidentified federal official as saying that the Budget Bureau was "the only device yet found to defend the President against his natural enemies— the cabinet officers."

Writing of Charles Zwick, Mayo's predecessor, Stewart Alsop has said: "His is one of the most powerful and least-known jobs in the Executive Branch." Alsop noted that although the budget director was not a member of the cabinet, "a very good case could be made for the proposition that the budget director ranks in terms of real power ahead of the Secretary of the Treasury and every other cabinet officer except the Secretaries of State and Defense." [8]

Operation of Federal Budget System

THE FEDERAL BUDGET is a relatively new institution of government. The first Secretary of the Treasury, Alexander Hamilton, tried briefly to coordinate Executive Branch money proposals, but his plan was soon abandoned. Through the succeeding years the various agencies of government dealt directly with congressional committees on their indi-

---

[8] Stewart Alsop, *The Center* (1968), pp. 259, 264.

vidual budgets. During most of the 19th century, with the exception of the Civil War period, federal revenues came mainly from customs duties and grew faster than expenditures.

These conditions prevailed until toward the end of the century, when the Spanish-American War and new demands for federal services began to produce deficits. The government went into debt in 10 of the 16 fiscal years between 1894 and 1909. Muckrakers of the period, agitating for reforms, prompted President Taft to appoint in 1910 a Commission on Economy and Efficiency. The commission's report, two years later, urged that a federal budget system be set up.

The recommended action was finally taken under the terms of the Budget and Accounting Act of 1921. That legislation (1) directed the President to prepare and submit to Congress an annual budget giving complete information on the condition of revenues and expenditures; (2) created the Bureau of the Budget to act as agent of the President in preparing the budget; and (3) created the General Accounting Office as an arm of Congress to review government spending. "This piece of legislation has been considered the most important fiscal reform enacted in the United States in the 20th century," the Tax Foundation has observed. "Prior to this time the United States, alone among the important nations of the world, had not developed a system of over-all national government budgeting." [9]

The first budget director, Charles G. Dawes, in the words of his successors, "marked out a limited area of responsibility, and for more than a decade after he left office [in 1922] the bureau held pretty much to the Dawes pattern. . . . The bureau as we know it today was formed in the later half of the Thirties." [10] Franklin D. Roosevelt began using the Budget Bureau "in coordinating the activities of the governmental agencies, rather than relying upon it strictly for . . . holding down government expenditures—which had been almost its sole function under his predecessors." [11]

At Roosevelt's insistence, Congress passed the Administrative Reorganization Act of 1939, which removed the bureau from the Treasury to the newly established Executive

[9] Tax Foundation, *Controlling Federal Expenditures*, December 1963, p. 9.

[10] Budget Director David E. Bell in speech on June 9, 1961, the 40th anniversary of President Harding's approval of the Budget and Accounting Act.

[11] A. J. Wann, "Franklin D. Roosevelt and the Bureau of the Budget," *Business and Government Review*, March-April 1968, p. 33.

Office of the President. Until that time, the bureau had had an average of only 38 to 42 staff members. Expansion, required to perform the new duties placed on the bureau by Roosevelt and by the coming of World War II, soon began. But even today the agency is small by Washington standards; it had 544 employees and a budget of $4.5 million in fiscal 1968. Its power has nevertheless continued to grow.

PROCESS OF BUDGET MAKING IN EXECUTIVE BRANCH

The visible part of the Budget Bureau's work is the annual budget which the President is required to submit to Congress. But that is only the tip of the iceberg. In a typical year, the major agencies and departments submit their separate "financial plans" to the bureau by May 1 for the fiscal year beginning 14 months later. Bureau examiners assigned to the various agencies review the proposals in May and June and report their findings to the budget director. During this time, other bureau specialists are consulting the Treasury Department and the Council of Economic Advisers about the long-range effects of agency programs on fiscal guidelines set forth in the latest federal budget.

After all this information has been accumulated and digested, the budget director begins discussions with the President on the shape of the future budget. These talks tend to become increasingly more frequent as the end of the year approaches and hard decisions can no longer be postponed. In the meantime, the director and his assistants have been asking department heads to justify their proposals.

"As guardians of the public purse, the Budget Bureau and Congress are expected to be more economy-minded than agency heads, who are responsible for the execution of specific programs," two experts have written. They add that on the other hand "agencies or departments rarely ask for all they feel they could use" because this might invite deep cuts and "set a precedent for the future." [12] Hence the agencies cannot aim too high or too low.

Step by step through the summer, the agencies fill in details in support of their programs and proposals. Finally—usually about September—they submit their budgets in final form to the Budget Bureau. Bureau examiners now conduct hearings, giving more attention than before to the basis of

---

[12] David J. Ott and Attiat F. Ott, *Federal Budget Policy* (Brookings Institution, 1965), p. 20.

cost estimates. Once again, they make recommendations to the director. He concentrates mostly on major items involving presidential policy, and identifies issues requiring a decision by the President himself. It is now late November or early December and the economic outlook has again been assessed by the bureau, the Treasury, and the Council of Economic Advisers. As final decisions are made one by one, the corresponding parts of the budget are committed to print. Until the last moment, cabinet members and other ranking government officials can appeal a decision to the President. "Occasionally an agency appeals," Charles L. Schultze told the House Appropriations Committee in budget hearings Jan. 31, 1966. Schultze, then the budget director, did not indicate how often the President reconsiders.

CHANGES IN REPORTING OF FEDERAL BUDGET DATA

The Budget of the United States Government for fiscal 1969, which President Johnson sent to Congress on Jan. 29, 1968, is about the size of a thick paperback novel. Its 556 pages are 116 more than in the budget of five years earlier, but it is trimmer than still earlier budgets. Prior to January 1962, federal budgets were as bulky as big-city telephone directories and filled with thousands of detailed schedules. Now these details are included in an appended volume, while the main budget document places greater emphasis than in past years on the relation of federal finances to conditions of the national economy. Graphs have been introduced to help in explaining the relationship. Similar changes have been made in the presidential budget message to Congress.

Each year since January 1950, the Bureau of the Budget has published an accompanying pamphlet titled *The Budget in Brief. Special Analyses* have also been published since 1942, dealing at various times with such matters as federal aid to state and local governments, federal credit programs, and federal research and development.

The fiscal 1963 budget presented for the first time an analysis of federal receipts and expenditures on a "National Income Accounts" basis. N.I.A., as it is called, includes an accounting of transactions in the multi-billion-dollar government trust funds, like those which finance the Social Security and interstate highway programs. These transactions do not appear in the so-called administrative budget— the budget which for years was best known to the public.

UNIFIED AND ADMINISTRATIVE BUDGET COMPARISONS

(Original estimates in billions of dollars)

UNIFIED BUDGET

Fiscal year	Expenditures	Revenues	Deficit
1968	175.6	155.8	19.8*
1969	186.0	178.0	8.0**

ADMINISTRATIVE BUDGET

1968	137.3	118.6	18.6
1969	147.5	135.6	11.9

* Actual deficit at end of fiscal year was $25.2 billion.
** On Dec. 19, 1968, President Johnson forecast a "small" surplus.

For the first time, in January 1967, the N.I.A. budget was stressed in a presidential message to Congress. President Johnson was able to place the projected deficit in fiscal 1968 at a lower figure by citing it rather than the administrative budget. He was scolded in the press for "budgetary sleight of hand" but won praise from leading fiscal experts who thought that the N.I.A. budget gave the truest account of the actual state of federal finances.

The confusion over budgets continued, however, and in October 1967 a presidentially appointed Commission on Budget Concepts recommended a "unified summary budget statement . . . to replace the three or more competing concepts." The third concept was that of a "consolidated cash budget," which was widely regarded by economists as best for measuring the budget's impact on the economy. The 16-member bipartisan commission was headed by David M. Kennedy, now the incoming Secretary of the Treasury, and is sometimes called the Kennedy Commission.

Its major recommendations were used in the 1969 budget, which (1) included trust fund revenues and expenditures; (2) determined total outlays by adding expenditures to net lending (the difference between what the government loaned the public and what it was repaid) ; and (3) presented expenditures and lending separately. The new accounting method made the budget more understandable but comparisons with prior budgets more difficult.

LACK OF UNIFIED BUDGETARY ACTION IN CONGRESS

Changes in budget making in the Executive Branch have not been accompanied by changes in budget review by the Legislative Branch. Congress considers the budget piecemeal; taxes and expenditures are decided separately by separate committees in each house. "The United States is now the only major nation . . . in which the Legislative Branch in effect makes a budget of its own, through its actions in examining and approving parts of the budget submitted by the Executive Branch." [13] Under the British parliamentary system, for example, the House of Commons must either accept the budget presented by the Cabinet or force the government to resign.

Thirteen Appropriations subcommittees of the House and 14 of the Senate individually consider specific areas of the budget, like defense or agriculture, in considerable isolation from one another.

> Members specializing in one particular type of spending may be relatively unfamiliar with, and at times unconcerned with, other programs. . . . They come to have something of a proprietary interest in their completed work, and as a rule it is not overridden by the full committee.
>
> The House almost always approves an appropriation bill as reported out by the committee. . . . In both the House and Senate, members who are not on the appropriations committees tend to be extremely hesitant to question committee recommendations.[14]

The House passed eight of 17 major appropriations bills in 1968 by voice vote, and the Senate seven. Individual lawmakers frequently have little chance to study committee hearings before a bill reaches the floor for a vote. *Congressional Quarterly* counted 332 meetings of the House Appropriations Committee and its subcommittees in 1968. All were closed, as is customary in the lower chamber. The Senate Appropriations Committee and its subcommittees met 139 times in open session in 1968 and 53 times in closed session.[15] All committees are required to distribute printed hearings and reports three days before floor debate, but the rule is frequently waived by unanimous consent in House and Senate.

The House Appropriations Committee has the reputation of being the more severe of the two in examining spending proposals. The Senate Appropriations Committee is considered something of an appellate tribunal or board of review. Agencies often plead with it to restore funds slashed by the House.

Congress has made several attempts, but with only a

---

[13] Tax Foundation, *op. cit.*, p. 20.

[14] *Ibid.*, p. 22.

[15] See *CQ Weekly Report*, Nov. 8, 1968, pp. 3103-3105.

modicum of success, to change the way it reviews the federal budget. The Legislative Reorganization Act of 1946 provided for a Joint Committee on the Legislative Budget, which was to consider the budget early in each session and recommend an annual ceiling on appropriations in light of prevailing economic conditions. The committee was unable to agree on a ceiling in 1947; when agreement was reached on a ceiling in 1948, Congress paid no heed. Soon afterward the committee fell into disuse.

The Omnibus Appropriations Act of 1950 authorized Congress to consolidate all general appropriations into one bill. But after a single trial, consolidation was abandoned in 1951. The Senate in 1967 passed another legislative reorganization bill, which proposed that (1) the President submit a revised budget June 1, reflecting changes in prior estimates; (2) committees hold open hearings on all except national security matters; and (3) roll-call votes be required on all appropriations bills. But in the House opposition arose among senior members and House Speaker John W. McCormack (D Mass.) sent the measure to the Rules Committee, where it died when the 1968 session ended. Legislation to revise rules in Congress encounters the opposition of ranking committee members who fear loss of influence over specific areas of interest.

WITHHOLDING OF APPROPRIATIONS BY BUDGET BUREAU

Congress in 1951 gave the Budget Bureau extensive authority to withhold funds from an agency after they had been appropriated. This device promotes central control over the timing and direction of government spending and helps to prevent an agency from spending faster than Congress intended. But it can also be used to impede a program that is popular with Congress but not with the White House. That happened in 1968 when Congress instructed the Johnson administration to cut expenses by $6 billion. In one of the economy moves which followed, the Budget Bureau withheld 20 per cent of federal funds for "impacted" schools— those educating large numbers of children of government workers and military personnel. The withholding affected many constituencies. Congress responded to their complaints by exempting impacted school funds from the economy drive.

The Budget Bureau contends that its control over release of funds is important because the budget is confined to fixed dates, July 1 to June 30, while the spending process is not rigid. Suppose that Congress authorizes an agency to spend $10 million in fiscal 1969 to set up a new program but is late in appropriating that amount. The agency has time to write checks for only $5 million before the fiscal year ends. Hence there is a $5 million carryover. This process may repeat itself year after year in scores of agencies.

Assume also that Congress authorized the same agency to spend $20 million in each of the two following fiscal years to continue the program. Even if the entire program had originally been requested in the President's 1969 budget, the two $20 million amounts would not have been reflected in the budget totals that year—only the $10 million initial outlay. Commenting on this practice, the United States Chamber of Commerce said: "The fact that the 1969 budget estimates the government will spend $186 billion is important. From the standpoint of spending control, however, it is more important that the President is asking authority from Congress to commit the government to spend $201 billion both in 1969 and later." [16]

Budget Choices After the Viet Nam War

A POLICY DEBATE is shaping up over whether defense or domestic needs have first claim on any potential surplus in the federal budget once fighting ceases in Viet Nam and the bulk of American forces are withdrawn. Budget planners speak of a "fiscal dividend" accruing from the normal revenue increases of an expanding national economy, combined with an expected decline in war costs. Charles Schultze, a former budget director (1965-68), tried to calculate the size of the probable dividend in a report he prepared for the Brookings Institution. The report appears in a book, *Agenda for the Nation,* which he and other specialists at Brookings compiled for the guidance of the incoming President.

Schultze estimated that in normal course the total revenue of the federal government would increase by $15.5 billion in fiscal 1969 and by the same amount in fiscal 1970—a figure somewhat above the oft-quoted $12 billion in fiscal 1968—

---

[16] *Here's the Issue* (biweekly publication of Legislative Department, United States Chamber of Commerce), Feb. 9, 1968.

and would increase by $18.5 billion in each of the three following fiscal years. But he concluded that the actual dividend would be smaller, ranging from zero in fiscal 1969 to perhaps $10 billion in fiscal 1971, because of built-in expenditure increases.

By Schultze's reckoning, Nixon will have only slight leeway for new expenditures before the last budget year of his first term. This appraisal was based on the assumption that fighting in Viet Nam would stop early in 1969 and that American troops would begin withdrawing by midyear. On the other hand, revenue from the surtax beyond mid-1969 was omitted from the calculations.

Rep. Henry S. Reuss (D Wis.), a member of the congressional Joint Economic Committee, forsees the possibility of a fiscal dividend of as much as $42 billion when the war ends. In House speeches, the liberal Democrat has said that annual military expenditures could be reduced by about $20 billion a year, cutting the annual defense budget to the neighborhood of $60 billion. The remainder of the dividend Reuss envisions would result from revenue-producing tax reforms, together with the normal revenue gains from economic expansion.

However, Maurice H. Stans has observed: "Defense spending tends to rise to a new plateau with each war or international emergency and never settles back to the prewar level. That will probably occur again." [17] Ralph E. Lapp, the physicist and author, has asserted that "it will take a strong-willed Secretary of Defense backed up by a resolute President" to bring the defense budget back down to a pre-Viet Nam level of $50 billion.[18] Defense-minded congressmen argue that costly weapons systems deferred because of wartime budgetary considerations must be built as soon as funds can be found. They maintain that it is an illusion to expect that the bulk of war "savings" from Viet Nam will become available to combat social ills.

Nixon Pledge of American Military Superiority

Close associates of Nixon have indicated that he plans to make good on his campaign promises to spend substantially

---

[17] Quoted by *U. S. News & World Report*, Nov. 25, 1968, p. 40.

[18] Ralph E. Lapp, "Cutting the Defense Budget," *New Republic*, Sept. 28, 1968, p. 28. Lapp is author of *The Weapons Culture* (1968), a book in which he contends that the "military-industrial" complex has grown enormously in size and influence since President Eisenhower warned of its power in his farewell speech of Jan. 17, 1961.

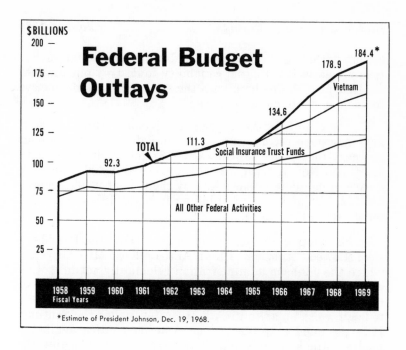

Federal Budget Outlays

$BILLIONS

200 —
175 —
150 —
125 —
100 —
75 —
50 —
25 —

TOTAL
92.3
111.3
134.6
178.9
184.4*

Vietnam

Social Insurance Trust Funds

All Other Federal Activities

1958 1959 1960 1961 1962 1963 1964 1965 1966 1967 1968 1969
Fiscal Years

*Estimate of President Johnson, Dec. 19, 1968.

more for defense. In a radio address over the CBS network on Oct. 24, Nixon spoke of a "security gap" in the nation's defenses and promised to bridge it before the United States encountered a "survival gap" in the early 1970s. Some Democrats dismissed "security gap" talk as campaign rhetoric, suggesting that the nominee was retaliating for their allegation in 1960 that the outgoing Eisenhower administration had allowed a "missile gap" to develop. The missile-gap issue was thought to have contributed to John F. Kennedy's defeat of Nixon for the presidency that year. Democrats later conceded that they had been wrong—that America had not fallen behind Russia in missile-building.

Nixon's appointment of Melvin R. Laird as Secretary of Defense soon made believers of some of the skeptics. Laird, as a Republican congressman from Wisconsin, has been a strong supporter of American military might and a zealous anti-Communist. Like Nixon, he wants to achieve and maintain a clear-cut military "superiority" over Russia—in contrast to the concept of an arms "parity" as advocated by Robert S. McNamara when he was Secretary of Defense. In his 1968 "defense posture" statement to Congress, McNamara said: "To put it bluntly, neither the Soviet Union nor the United States can attack the other, even by surprise

action, without suffering massive damage in retaliation. . . .
It is precisely this mutual capability to destroy one another
. . . that provides us both with the strongest possible motive
to avoid a strategic nuclear war."

On the eve of the Nov. 5 election, Nixon's campaign staff
gave newsmen estimates of a rise in defense spending over
the next four years to a peak of $87 billion in the fourth
year. The Nov. 4 estimates also projected a $26 billion in-
crease in non-defense spending by then. That would mean a
total budget of about $220 billion in fiscal 1973, about $35
billion more than in fiscal 1969.

In his campaign book, *Nixon on the Issues,* the President-
elect showed enthusiasm for an Anti-Ballistic Missile system
which the Johnson administration reluctantly set in motion
under congressional pressure. Over the bitter opposition of
its liberal members, Congress approved $1.2 billion in 1968
to begin work on a "thin" A.B.M. system called the Sentinel.
It is designed to protect some American cities against a
nuclear attack from China. Cost estimates of enlarging the
system to provide protection from a Soviet missile attack as
well range from $40 billion to $60 billion.

Critics in Congress and the Pentagon argue that Sentinel
will be the least effective and most expensive weapons system
ever built. Nixon is expected to push A.B.M. development at
a gradual pace because of tight budgets and a desire to weigh
its potential benefits against other defense concepts. One
rival concept is the Navy's proposed Seaborne Anti-Ballistic
Missile Intercept System, or SAMBIS. It envisions submarines
lying in wait off enemy coasts ready to shoot down intercon-
tinental missiles with seaborne intercept missiles. Nixon is
reported to be attracted to the idea. He is portrayed as being
interested also in developing a new strategic bomber to replace the Air Force's aging B-52s and B-58s, and new tac-
tical aircraft for the Air Force and Navy. Nixon said in
campaign speeches that he wanted an all-volunteer army,
which defense officials estimate would be costlier to maintain
than the present part-conscript army.

UNCERTAIN FATE OF MCNAMARA'S SYSTEMS ANALYSIS

Nixon has repeatedly criticized decision-making in the
Pentagon during the McNamara era and has left in suspense
the question of whether the "systems analysis" approach to
defense spending will be discarded. He said in his "security

gap" speech that the McNamara "whiz kids" had made wrong decisions through their computerized evaluations.

The system of Planning, Programing and Budgeting (P.P.B.), which McNamara and Assistant Defense Secretary Alain C. Enthoven installed at the Pentagon was held up as a model for all major departments of government during the Johnson presidency. Johnson directed the executive agencies on Aug. 25, 1965, to see whether the Pentagon system could be adapted to their needs. But the system was unpopular with many high military officers and with some senior members of defense committees in Congress. Both groups felt that their influence had been reduced by its existence.[19]

Enthoven, defending the system before a House Government Operations subcommittee on Sept. 27, 1967, said that before it began functioning in 1961 "the defense budget was based on a predetermined financial ceiling." That ceiling, he said, was based on judgments about the nation's capacity to pay, "but without specific reference to military strategy or requirements." Others have suggested that the total defense sum was then apportioned among the three military services largely on the basis of their lobbying ability in Congress. It is not likely that Nixon will revert to the pre-1961 system, but he may put less emphasis on "systems analysis" in the Pentagon to make it more palatable to congressional and military critics.

PLANS FOR TAX INCENTIVES AND FOR REVENUE SHARING

On the domestic side, the Nixon fiscal blueprint of Nov. 4 looked into the future for four years. Its estimate of a $26 billion increase in non-defense spending included direct federal spending in racial ghettos and higher Social Security and Medicare benefits. There would also be tax credits amounting to $7 billion a year for four years to encourage private industry to make investments in the ghettos and train the hard-core unemployed.

Nixon made tax incentives a key feature of his domestic proposals. After his election, he apparently softened the opposition of House Ways and Means Chairman Wilbur D. Mills (D Ark.). Mills conferred with Nixon in New York on Dec. 4 and, hours later, omitted portions of a prepared speech which attacked tax credits as a means of "backdoor financing." In extemporaneous remarks to his audience, the Na-

---

[19] See "Defense Spending Management," *E.R.R.*, 1966 Vol. II, pp. 787-804.

tional Association of Manufacturers, Mills indicated that he and Nixon had agreed that any tax credits which Congress might authorize would be treated as expenditures in the federal budget. At present, there is no formal accounting of revenue losses from tax credits. On his part, Mills promised to consider bills to allow tax credits to businesses engaged in training the jobless; he did not say what he thought about tax credits for other purposes. No recent President has been able to obtain enactment of tax legislation opposed by Mills.

Sharing of federal tax revenues with the states is a long-standing Republican aim that will probably be deferred until the federal budget picture brightens. Through revenue sharing, a fixed portion of federally collected taxes would be turned back to the states without strings attached.[20] The concept was given prominence during the Kennedy administration by Walter W. Heller, chairman of the Council of Economic Advisers. Since then, Republicans have endorsed the idea more heartily than Democrats. Many big-city mayors have opposed it on the ground that state capitols have short-changed cities for years and cannot be entrusted to do better. The nation's governors, however, have repeatedly expressed their approval.

A more immediate prospect is that of offering major federal aid to the states in the form of "block grants." Congress in 1968 overrode objections of the Johnson administration and voted to apportion crime-fighting funds among the states in lump sums. This provision of the Omnibus Crime Control and Safe Streets Act of 1968 marked a departure from the time-honored method of allocating specific funds to local communities for specific projects. The new method gives political leverage to the statehouse rather than to a federal agency in Washington.

The attitude of a Democratic-controlled Congress is a critical factor in almost all of the President-elect's economic programs. "If there is one thing clear from the experience of the last three years," Robert T. Elson of *Fortune* has written, "it is that the problem of managing the economy is less one of economics than of politics." [21] The uncertainty of future political decisions—at home or abroad—tends to cloud all long-range budgetary assumptions.

---

[20] See "Federal-State Revenue Sharing," *E.R.R.*, 1964 Vol. II, pp. 943-960.

[21] Robert T. Elson, "How the Old Politics Swamped the New Economics," *Fortune*, September 1968, p. 74.

Money Supply in Inflation

by

Hoyt Gimlin

1 9 6 9
Feb. 26

MONEY SUPPLY IN INFLATION

THE NATION entered its ninth year of uninterrupted economic growth in February 1969 with more to worry about than to cheer about. The longest span of prosperity in American history has spawned an inflation which sent consumer prices up 4.7 per cent in 1968, the biggest yearly rise in the cost of living since 1951. As the Nixon administration came into office announcing that inflation was its main economic concern, the country was already beginning to witness what an economist described as "a dramatic collision of two very powerful forces." Albert T. Sommers of the National Industrial Conference Board pointed out that in early 1969 "Business has been much stronger than was expected [last summer], and the strength of business has induced much tougher policy restraints." [1]

After waiting in vain since mid-1968 for the 10 per cent surcharge on income taxes to curb inflation, the Federal Reserve System in December took steps to decrease the money supply, tighten bank credit, and raise interest rates. It pushed up the basic rate on Federal Reserve lending to commercial banks—the discount rate—by one-half of a percentage point, to 5½ per cent, on Dec. 17. The nation's money supply increased at an annual rate of only 3.7 per cent in January, in contrast to the 6.5 per cent average for all of 1968. Reduction of the rate of increase was accomplished in part through sale of government securities—an action which has the effect of diminishing the lendable funds of commercial banks by several times more than the actual value of the securities sold. Between the year-end and early February, the Fed had disposed of a half-billion dollars' worth of its holdings of government securities.

The effect of these moves became apparent in the money markets. Major commercial banks on Jan. 8 raised their "prime" interest rate for the third time in less than six

---

[1] Albert T. Sommers, "The Great Confrontation," *The Conference Board Record* (monthly publication of the National Industrial Conference Board, February 1969), p. 4.

weeks, making their best customers pay a record 7 per cent on borrowings. Others paid more. George Romney, Secretary of Housing and Urban Development, on Jan. 24 raised the interest rate ceiling on government-backed mortgages to 7½ per cent, up from 6¾ per cent, in an effort to attract funds to the housing market. Some states elevated permissible rates under their usury laws to 8 per cent and beyond. The Treasury on Jan. 29 had to offer the highest yield (6.42 per cent) since the Civil War to sell notes maturing in only 15 months. Corporation bonds of the highest quality passed the 7 per cent mark in January, some of them bearing record high interest rates.

EXPECTED RESULTS OF BATTLE TO CURB INFLATION

By February, economists were talking about the "cumulative consequences" of the monetary restraints, of the surtax, and of the higher Social Security taxes which went into effect Jan. 1. Some were beginning to use words like "overkill," suggesting that the price of easing inflation might be a "mini-recession" and high unemployment. John R. Bunting, president of the First Pennsylvania Banking and Trust Company, Philadelphia, was quoted in the *New York Times* on Feb. 5 as saying that Federal Reserve officials themselves were worried for fear their tight-money campaign might be getting out of hand.

"Desirable as it might be to slow inflation without raising unemployment," the chief economist of the Philadelphia Federal Reserve Bank said recently, "this happy combination seems too much to expect." David P. Eastburn, the economist, said the Federal Reserve is being careful to apply restraints only gradually in an effort to hold "dislocations and layoffs" to a minimum. His remarks, reviewed in advance by the Federal Reserve Board staff in Washington, appeared in the February issue of his bank's publication *Business Review*.

Paul W. McCracken, chairman of the President's Council of Economic Advisers, appeared to approve the present degree of restraint. In Paris, where he was attending an international economic conference, McCracken told newsmen on Feb. 11: "In general, we are on the right course. The budget is back under control, and the course of monetary and credit policy is tracking about right." Testifying before the Joint Economic Committee of Congress on Feb. 17, McCracken described the economic outlook in these cautious

Money Supply in Inflation

AMERICAN PRICE INCREASES, 1958-68
(1957-59 = 100)

Year	Cost-of-living index	Year	Cost-of-living index
1958	100.7	1964	108.1
1959	101.5	1965	109.9
1960	103.1	1966	113.1
1961	104.2	1967	116.3
1962	105.4	1968	121.0
1963	106.7		

PRICE INCREASES ABROAD, 1958-68

	Per cent		Per cent
Britain	37	Japan	67
Canada	27	West Germany	26
France	52	United States	21
Italy	41		

terms: "We regard some slowing down of the rate of expansion in the first half of the year as probable, although the evidence is still uncertain." President Johnson and his economic advisers in their last report to Congress, in January, forecast a slowdown in the first half of 1969, allowing some easing of monetary restraints after the early part of the year. But McCracken disagreed with the premise that a first-half "cooling off" alone would be sufficient to keep inflation on a downward course.

In his first White House news conference, Jan. 27, President Nixon said he hoped inflation could be brought under control "without too much managing of the economy." He had in mind "some fine tuning of our fiscal and monetary affairs," and he specifically rejected a return to wage and price guidelines. The White House can exercise fiscal leverage through higher or lower spending of appropriated funds and through its budgetary and tax recommendations to Congress. Monetary controls reside almost exclusively in the hands of the Federal Reserve, which is independent in theory and sometimes in fact. However, officials of the Fed still have bitter memories of "going it alone" with monetary restraints in 1966 and of being blamed for the "credit crunch" that followed.

DEBATE OVER CAUSES OF THE INFLATIONARY SURGE

What had been a barely perceptible inflationary movement took an obvious upward turn in 1965—at about the time the United States escalated its military effort in Viet Nam. Con-

125

sumer prices climbed 5.5 per cent between mid-1965 and mid-1967, almost as much as in the preceding four years. Under the circumstances, the war became identified with inflation, although not all economists agree that it was the principal cause of inflation.

The word "inflation" is sometimes used to describe both higher prices and their causes. It may refer to an expansion of the money supply and of credit in excess of the supply of goods (monetary inflation); large deficits in the federal budget (fiscal inflation); an increase in prices out of proportion to an increase in costs (profits inflation); and an excess of labor costs over gains in productivity (wage inflation). The first two forms of inflation (monetary and fiscal) generate *demand-pull* pressures, which come from too much money chasing too few goods. Profits inflation and wage inflation contribute to *cost-push* pressures.

On the eve of President Johnson's departure from office, his Cabinet Committee on Price Stability made public a staff report attributing much of the recent inflationary surge to "oligopoly profits"—those of a few gigantic companies which dominate a single industry. A neo-Keynesian economist, Robert Lekachman, stated this thesis in 1966, when he wrote that the "Goliaths of manufacturing" tend to make huge profits without engaging in real price competition. ". . . In steel U. S. Steel, in automobiles General Motors—announce a set of prices which other companies conventionally follow." [2] High corporation profits, in turn, offer an inviting target for union wage demands and so a price-wage spiral may be set in motion.

John Kenneth Galbraith, the economist and author, said in a letter published in the *Washington Post* on Feb. 11, 1969, that by refusing to revive Kennedy-Johnson "guideposts," [3] Nixon was "sacrificing his only chance of reconciling price stability with high employment." [4] Galbraith added that "Whoever gave the President that line about 'fine-tuning' the economy with monetary and fiscal measures was guilty of a shameless snow job."

---

[2] Robert Lekachman, *The Age of Keynes* (1966), pp. 247-248.

[3] "Guideposts" or guidelines were established by the President's Council of Economic Advisers in 1962 in an attempt to persuade unions and employers to limit price and wage increases to 3.2 per cent a year, the average rate of productivity over the previous five years. The guidelines gradually fell into disuse under the pressure of growing inflation. See "Anti-inflation Policies in America and Britain," *E.R.R.*, 1965 Vol. II, pp. 921-938.

[4] In December and January only 3.3 per cent of the country's work force was unemployed—the smallest proportion since March 1953.

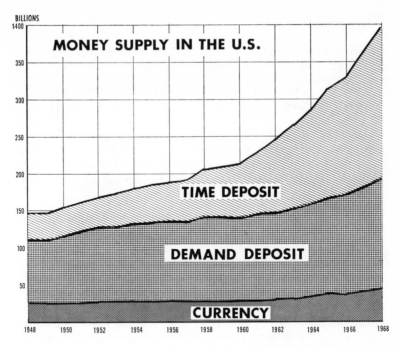

BILLIONS
$400

MONEY SUPPLY IN THE U.S.

350

300

250

200

150

TIME DEPOSIT

100

DEMAND DEPOSIT

50

CURRENCY

1948 1950 1952 1954 1956 1958 1960 1962 1964 1966 1968

The label "new economics" has been used to describe thinking in the 1960s in line with theories propounded by John Maynard Keynes (1883-1946), the British economist. In his *General Theory of Employment, Interest and Money* (1936) and other works, Keynes advocated planned budget deficits and tax cuts to stimulate a national economy and promote full employment. The principal American architects of that policy have been two chairmen of the Council of Economic Advisers, Walter W. Heller (1961-64) and Gardner Ackley (1964-68). Galbraith differed from them in that he favored higher public spending in preference to tax cuts.

FRIEDMAN'S THEORY ON GROWTH OF MONEY SUPPLY

Esteem for the "new economics" has suffered from the post-1965 inflation and from the initial failure of the 1968 surtax to slow it down. Even before the Nixon administration took office, official Washington was much concerned about the proper "mix" of monetary and fiscal controls. For a long time, monetary policy meant primarily control of interest rates and credit. But a different view had been traditional at the University of Chicago, where Prof. Milton Friedman developed the basic theory that the rate of growth

127

of the money supply is the key determinant of the direction and quality of economic change.

Monetary theorists of the "Chicago school" have gained a number of adherents in the past few years and now enjoy a respectful hearing in Washington. A congressional subcommittee reported on Dec. 29 that two-thirds of 71 leading economists whose views it had solicited favored making growth of the money supply the prime objective of monetary policy.[5] McCracken has described his own thinking as "Friedmanesque"—though not "Friedmanite."

Friedman has taken a more extreme position than most of his followers and has argued that monetary policy can be pursued independently of fiscal policy. He has won converts, or "half converts," to his advocacy of growth of the money supply at a pre-determined fixed rate. Money supply usually means currency in circulation plus demand deposits ("checkbook money") in banks, although some economists also include time deposits. The rate of growth, by either definition, has fluctuated from year to year. Friedman and other money supply theorists say that the growth rate could be controlled almost mechanically by the Federal Reserve, and that the economy could be left to run itself in a stable fashion with little or no interference from the government. In *A Monetary History of the United States* (1963), Friedman and co-author Anna Jacobson Schwartz portrayed the economic bad times of the country's past, including the Depression Thirties, as the result of sharp contractions in the money supply. Friedman updated this theme in his book *Dollars and Deficits,* published in 1968. He has suggested a 5 per cent growth rate as a desirable goal for the present period.

CRITICISM OF FEDERAL RESERVE MONETARY POLICY

Friedman's views have been in the ascendant at a time when one of his targets, Federal Reserve policy, has come increasingly under attack. For years the board and its financially conservative chairman, William McChesney Martin Jr., have incurred the wrath of Rep. Wright Patman (D Texas) whenever the Fed tightened credit. The ideological feud between Martin and Patman is one of the oldest in Washington. Other, more conservative, critics of the Fed have arisen since the 1966 "credit crunch." The *Wall Street Journal* commented editorially on Jan. 21, 1969: "A major aim of

---

[5] House Banking and Currency Subcommittee on Domestic Finance, *Compendium on Monetary Policy Guidelines and Federal Reserve Structure* (December 1968).

the Reserve System is supposed to be the promotion of economic stability. Yet the Fed, in its ineptitude, frequently became a source of instability." The newspaper said that as the money managers "worried intermittently about inflation and recession, they were inclined to shift with exceeding abruptness from restraint to ease, and vice versa." The Fed "moved with such suddenness in 1966 that it nearly triggered a money panic."

The Fed contends that it has been the victim rather than the villain—that in 1966 it tried to stem inflation without any help from Congress on the White House. If it became an "engine of inflation" in 1967 and 1968—as is sometimes said —it is because there were huge federal deficits to be financed, and it was compelled to pump new infusions of money into the economy in the process of financing them.[6]

BUDGET RECORD SINCE 1965

(billions of dollars)

Fiscal year	Surplus or deficit	Fiscal year	Surplus or deficit
1965	—3.4	1968	—25.2
1966	—2.2	1969*	2.4
1967	—9.9	1970*	3.4

* President Johnson's budget estimates.

Andrew F. Brimmer, a member of the Federal Reserve Board, has reported that federal borrowing accounted for only 5 per cent of the net funds raised on the nation's money markets in 1965, but for 18 per cent in 1967. During the first and third quarters of 1968 the figures rose to 33 and 27 per cent, respectively. The Federal Reserve expanded the volume of funds supplied directly to credit markets by only $3.8 billion in 1965, but in the first quarter of 1968 by $8.3 billion and in the third quarter by $10.2 billion. "With so much of the excess demand originating with the federal government," Brimmer said, "a decision not to permit some increase in bank credit would have subjected the money and capital markets to far more strains than it is reasonable to expect them to bear." [7]

In keeping with its new monetary restraints, the Fed in recent weeks has been selling rather than buying government securities. On Feb. 5 its ownership of government

---

[6] See "Federal Budget Making," *E.R.R.*, 1969 Vol. I, pp. 3-19, and "National Debt Management," *E.R.R.*, 1967 Vol. II, pp. 885-902.

[7] Speech before Joint Seminar of the Department of Economics and the Institute of Government and Public Affairs, University of California at Los Angeles, Jan. 10, 1969.

RESERVE OWNERSHIP OF NATIONAL DEBT

Year-end	Fed Ownership *(millions of dollars)*	Per cent of total
1960	27,248	9
1965	40,885	12
1967	48,891	14
1968	52,529	15

SOURCE: Data adapted from Treasury and Federal Reserve sources.

bonds, notes and the like stood at $52.0 billion, down from a record $53.4 billion in Nov. 1968. With the federal budget in balance, the Treasury will not have to borrow as extensively in 1969 as in 1968. However, securities that it has sold previously are maturing constantly and must be refinanced. The national debt (currently $364.2 billion) is, in effect, being refinanced in its entirety every four years.[8] When a Treasury refinancing operation—frequently a public auction —is not successful, the Fed usually steps in to buy the securities.

As if in rebuttal to the Fed's defense of its action, the First National City Bank of New York commented in its *Monthly Economic Letter* of January 1969: "The impact of Treasury operations on money and bank credit provides a good argument for improving fiscal policy, but it does not completely absolve the Federal Reserve of responsibility for the abnormal growth of money supply in the last two years." Friedman wrote in *Newsweek*, Jan. 20, 1969: "The plain fact is that inflation is made in Washington, in that stately and impressive Grecian temple on Constitution Avenue that houses the Board of Governors of the Federal Reserve System."

Federal Reserve and Monetary Controls

CONGRESS created the Federal Reserve System in 1913 as an official agency to control the quality and quantity of American money. The agency is a fusion of private enterprise and government that serves as a central bank. Most countries of the world have a single reserve bank, or central

---

[8] McCracken told the Joint Economic Committee on Feb. 17 that he hoped that the "debt structure" could be lengthened. In recent years only short-term securities have been sold because of a ceiling of 4¼ per cent on interest paid on bonds of seven years' duration or longer.

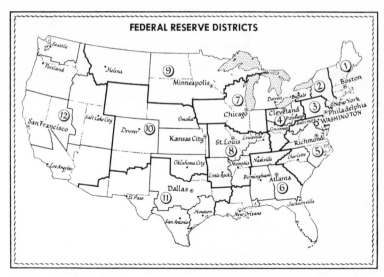

FEDERAL RESERVE DISTRICTS

bank, but the United States has a regional system of 12 districts, each with a Federal Reserve Bank. There are also 24 Federal Reserve Bank branches serving specific areas within the districts. The 36 banks and branches form the middle layer of a three-tier pyramid.

At the base are the member banks of the Federal Reserve System—5,978 on Jan. 1, 1969. They account for fewer than half of the 13,679 commercial banks in the United States, but they control about 85 per cent of the total assets. The Federal Reserve System includes all 4,716 national banks—those federally chartered—and 1,262 state banks that have qualified for, and chosen, membership. Within the system, 182 major banks in 50 national and regional financial centers are designated city banks. All other members are country banks.

At the apex of the pyramid is the Board of Governors in Washington, consisting of seven members appointed by the President with the approval of the Senate. The governors are selected for 14-year terms and are ineligible for reappointment after having served a full term.[9] No two governors may come from the same district. The chairman and vice chairman are designated by the President from among the board members for four-year terms and may be re-designated.

[9] However, they can be named more than once to less-than-full terms. William McChesney Martin Jr. was appointed in 1951 to fill an unexpired term and in 1956 to a full 14-year term (ending Feb. 1, 1970). Martin was designated chairman at the outset and has been re-appointed chairman at four-year intervals.

MEMBER BANK RESERVE REQUIREMENTS

Type of deposit and class of bank	Minimum-maximum required by law	Legal ratio in effect
Demand deposits		
Reserve city	10-22%	16.5%*
Reserve country	7-14	12*
Time deposits		
All Reserve banks	3-10	3**

* One-half per cent more on deposits in excess of $5 million.
** Six per cent on deposits in excess of $5 million.
Adapted from Federal Reserve data.

DEVICES TO CONTROL CREDIT AND MONEY SUPPLY

The Fed employs an assortment of devices to influence economic activity beyond the realm of "just banking." It can act to ease or tighten credit, enlarge or diminish the money supply, and raise or lower interest rates. Usually these things work in combination, but not always. From August 1965 to April 1966 the money supply expanded at a faster rate than in the preceding 12 months, and more business loans were being made, but at the same time interest rates rose. Warning that "easing" and "tightening" are semantic traps, economist Henry C. Wallich noted: "By the money supply and bank credit test, monetary policy was easy; by the interest test it tightened." [10]

Perhaps the best known economic lever available to the Fed is the *discount rate*. It is the rate of interest commercial banks pay when they borrow from Federal Reserve banks. Technically, changes in the discount rate are made independently by each of the 12 Reserve banks but, in practice, rates are raised and lowered at about the same time everywhere upon the initiative of the Board of Governors.

The discount rate frequently is used to signal a shift in policy. When it is raised, interest rates tend to go up across the country—particularly the rates on short-term loans. Conversely, a lowering of the discount rate is usually followed by lower-price credit in the money markets. The *prime rate*, the rate of interest commercial banks charge their best customers, tends to move up and down in relation to the discount rate, always a point or so higher.

The monetary tool with the most immediate and widespread effect is the board's power to vary the *reserve require-*

[10] Speech before Symposium on Money, Interest Rates and Economic Activity, sponsored by American Bankers Association, Washington, D. C., April 6, 1967.

ments of member banks. A change in the reserve requirements alters the ratio of cash reserves which member banks
must keep in relation to deposits. Lowering the ratio has the
effect of immediately making more of the bank's money
available for lending, and raising it has the reverse effect.

Because reserves produce no income, banks try to keep
them close to the required minimum. Yet they will incur
penalty charges if reserves fall below the line. Member
banks have several ways of avoiding deficiencies. They may
borrow reserve balances for brief periods from banks that
have excess reserves. Since World War II, this "federal funds
market" has become a medium for making financial dealings
far more extensive than the mere redistribution of bank
reserves. By making full use of this market, the banks supply
themselves with more lendable funds and become more willing lenders.[11]

Member banks may also protect themselves against un-
foreseen reserve losses by holding short-term government
securities and other liquid assets which they can sell quickly,
if necessary. They may likewise borrow from their district
Reserve bank, a practice known to bankers as going to the
"discount window." Discounting — lending — was actively
practiced during the first two decades of the Fed's existence
but fell into disuse in the 1930s, when banks accumulated
large reserves and were making few loans. The marginal
role of the discount window was formally recognized in
1955 by a change in Fed regulations; borrowing was to be
limited to assistance during peaks of temporary, seasonal or
emergency needs. In short, the board frowned on borrowing.

Later, its thinking changed. The Federal Reserve in 1968
made public a three-year study proposing that banks be
allowed to borrow at will, up to specified limits.[12] It also
proposed more frequent, and smaller, changes in the discount
rate to keep it more closely aligned with market conditions
and to make the changes less dramatic. Frequent and minute
changes in the discount rate, perhaps only one-eighth of a
percentage point, presumably would become an instrument
of "fine tuning." In 27 discount rate changes in the past 14
years, all except one have been by one-half of a percentage

---

[11] See *The Federal Funds Market* (published by Federal Reserve Bank of Boston,
third edition, 1968).

[12] "Reappraisal of the Federal Reserve Discount Mechanism," *Federal Reserve
Bulletin*, July 1968, pp. 545-551.

point. The exception was a one-fourth of a percentage point change in August 1968. Board member George W. Mitchell told the Joint Economic Committee of Congress, Sept. 11, 1968, that under the proposal the discount mechanism would assume greater importance, but he added that "I should emphasize that open-market operations are still envisioned as the main tool of monetary policy." [13]

OPERATION OF FEDERAL OPEN MARKET COMMITTEE

Presidents of the 12 Reserve banks go to Washington about every three weeks to sit down with the Board of Governors at a meeting of the Federal Open Market Committee—the principal agency for setting monetary policy. All seven members of the board and five of the 12 presidents are members of the committee. Although the other presidents customarily attend the meetings, they have no vote. The chairman of the Board of Governors is chairman also of the F.O.M.C., as the committee is known, and the president of the New York Reserve Bank is vice chairman.

The committee meets in closed sessions, and its decisions are not announced. An official record of the meeting is published about 90 days later in the monthly *Federal Reserve Bulletin* and in an annual report. "By the time the document appears," the *Morgan Guaranty Survey* has noted, "the effect of any change in monetary policy has become apparent in the market. The account given, moreover, tends to be terse in style, with little inkling of the give-and-take of debate leading to policy decisions." [14] The Joint Economic Committee has complained of the "vagueness and obscurity" of F.O.M.C. reports.

The F.O.M.C., by deciding when the Federal Reserve System should buy and sell government securities, influences a broad range of economic activity. The national money supply is expanded and contracted by these purchases and sales —regardless of who sells government securities to the Fed or who buys them from it. If the Fed buys $1 million of Treasury bills from a New York dealer in government securities, it pays for them with a check issued on itself.

[13] The Joint Economic Committee on Feb. 5, 1969, asked that the proposed changes not be put into effect until it had had more time to study them. Rep. Patman, the committee chairman, said that to afford banks easier access to reserves would give them an unfair advantage over savings and loan associations, which do not have the same borrowing rights. Patman noted that if S & L's, which provide much of the country's mortgage money, suffer, so does the housing market.

[14] "Opening the Books on Monetary Policy," *Morgan Guaranty Survey* (monthly publication of Morgan Guaranty Trust Co. of New York, March 1965), p. 3.

The dealer deposits the check in his account at a commercial bank. The bank sends it in for collection, and upon clearance it is credited with $1 million in its reserve account at a Federal Reserve bank.

In this way the government "creates" money. Expansion of the money supply does not stop there, however. The commercial bank which received the check has an added million dollars in reserves. It is now entitled to make loans up to about six times that amount. (Though *fractional reserves* vary, 6 to 1 is the approximate reserve-lending ratio of city member banks.) In a reverse process, carried to its theoretical limits, the Fed can shrink the money supply about $7 million by selling $1 million worth of securities.

USE OF 'OPEN MOUTH' POLICY AND MORAL SUASION

The three classic tools for implementing monetary policy thus are *open market operations,* changes in the *discount rate,* and changes in *reserve requirements.* The *London Economist* recently pointed to still a fourth technique—that of "open mouth policy."

> Lately the money managers have been working the jawbone overtime. The problem is that, while the central bank has managed to tighten credit in an active campaign over the past seven weeks or so, it is afraid to bear down much more vigorously for fear of oversqueezing as it did in 1966. So the Fed's spokesmen are trying to convince businessmen that credit is tighter than it really is.[15]

The Fed prefers the phrase "moral suasion" to "open mouth." Moral suasion is used to describe the twilight zone where control comes more from suggestion than from specific action. An example occurred during the Korean War when President Truman asked the board to encourage and coordinate voluntary agreements among financial institutions to hold back credit expansion. "The most spectacular success of this program was in the refusal of investment bankers to handle state bonds issued for the purpose of paying a veterans' bonus." [16]

Another set of controls under the supervision of the Board of Governors deals not with credit in general, nor with moral suasion, but with control over a specific kind of credit—that of bank lending to finance transactions in the stock market. This type of control does not operate through

---

15 "Fed's Open Mouth," *The Economist,* Feb. 1, 1969, p. 41.
16 Walter W. Haines, *Money Prices and Policy* (1966), p. 250.

the reserve position of member banks. Instead, the board specifies the down payment required to finance purchases of securities listed on national exchanges. These *margin requirements* are fixed currently at 80 per cent on listed securities and 60 per cent on listed bonds that can be converted into stocks. Congress in 1968 gave the Fed similar authority to set margin requirements on over-the-counter stock purchases. These requirements are now being written.

Limits on Federal Reserve Independence

THE FEDERAL RESERVE is an independent agency, within limits. Its powers, delegated by Congress in the Federal Reserve Act of 1913, which established the system, were enlarged by the Banking Act of 1935. But Congress is fond of pointing out that what it gives, it can also take away. The Fed's degree of independence underlies its relations with the Banking and Currency committees of the Senate and House and with the Joint Economic Committee. The last two committees are under the chairmanship of Rep. Patman, who has proposed legislation to strip the Fed of much of its independence.

One bill, re-introduced by Patman in the 91st Congress, would (1) reduce the number of members of the board to five and their terms of office to five years; (2) require the board to coordinate open market operations with economic policies and programs of the President "pursuant to the Employment Act" of 1946, which make it public policy to "promote maximum employment, production and purchasing power"; (3) compel the President to submit guidelines on monetary policy in his annual economic message to Congress; and (4) make funds to operate the Federal Reserve System subject to congressional appropriation. The system now is self-financing.

During hearings on an identical measure in 1968, Patman gained the support of Milton Friedman, in principle if not in particulars. "I am opposed to independence for the Federal Reserve System," Friedman wrote Patman. But McCracken, whose views were also solicited, said "It is desirable to have our monetary authority have some degree of remoteness from immediate political pressures." [17] A spokesman for the House Banking and Currency Committee said it was not known now whether Patman would assign his bill a high priority and try to push it through the present Congress.

The Joint Economic Committee last year asked the Fed, beginning in 1969, to give it a special explanation in writing whenever the money supply in any quarter expands at a rate of more than 6 per cent or less than 2 per cent. One of the most prestigious business groups in the nation, the Committee for Economic Development, endorsed the 2-6 per cent range in a report issued Jan. 30, 1969.[18] Project director Eli Shapiro, a Harvard professor, said that the C.E.D. did not necessarily agree with Friedman that growth of the money supply should be put on "automatic pilot." It did, however, favor limiting the Fed's discretionary powers.

It is still uncertain whether the Federal Reserve will follow the Joint Committee's advice. Rep. Henry S. Reuss (D Wis.) complained in 1968 that the "dialogue between the Joint Economic Committee, in its annual reports, and the Federal Reserve System, in the minutes of the Open Market Committee, might as well have been conducted in Urdu on the one side and Swahili on the other."

Treasury-Fed Dispute and Recessions of 1950s

Chairman Martin is known to place high value on the Fed's independence. It can be argued that the Fed lost its independence to the Treasury during World War II and regained it only in 1951, when Martin left the Treasury as assistant secretary and came to the Fed as its chairman. He had been instrumental in negotiating the famous "accord"—understanding—between the Treasury and the Federal Reserve which went into effect a few days before he became chairman.

The Treasury-Federal Reserve dispute originated in World War II, when it was the policy of the Fed to support the prices of government securities and thus to keep down interest rates on federal obligations issued to finance budget deficits. Continuation of the arrangement into the period when the postwar economy was gathering momentum made the Fed, in former F.R.B. Chairman Marriner S. Eccles's

---

[17] House Banking and Currency Subcommittee on Domestic Finance, *op. cit.*, pp. 203, 472.

[18] *Fiscal and Monetary Policies for Steady Economic Growth.*

YEARLY CHANGES IN MONEY SUPPLY AND G.N.P.

(in percentages)

Year	Money supply	G.N.P.	Year	Money supply	G.N.P.
1953	1.1	5.5	1961	3.7	3.3
1954	2.7	0.1	1962	1.4	7.7
1955	2.2	9.1	1963	3.8	5.4
1956	1.3	5.3	1964	4.1	7.1
1957	—.7	5.2	1965	4.7	8.3
1958	3.8	1.4	1966	2.2	9.2
1959	.6	8.1	1967	6.4	5.6
1960	—.6	4.1	1968	6.5	9.0

Adapted from Federal Reserve and Commerce Department data.

oft-quoted phrase, "an engine of inflation." The new inflationary surge that accompanied the Korean War finally brought the Treasury-Fed dispute to a head. The Fed then adopted a "bills only" policy; it would confine its open market operations to short-term Treasury bills, except when "a disorderly situation in the government securities market" required it to intervene in support of long-term issues.

The "bills only" policy was abandoned in February 1961 because of growing problems with the balance of international payments. During the 1950s the Fed was caught in a policy conflict. The international payments deficit, together with a modest inflation at home, seemed to call for contraction of the money supply. But the country's slow economic growth seemed to call for expansion of the money supply. The Federal Reserve gave priority to contraction through restrictive policies which, in the view of some economists, led to the recessions of 1953, 1957 and 1959. From the early 1960s until mid-1966, monetary policy was expansive in terms of growth of the money supply, though interest rates edged upward. The period was one of the nation's most successful in terms of sustained economic growth and price stability. But monetary policy was viewed as too expansive in terms of the balance of payments—or not expansive enough in terms of unemployment.[19]

RESISTANCE OF BANKERS TO FED CREDIT TIGHTENING

The Federal Reserve's freedom of action is circumscribed by events, if not by formal commitment. Within hours of Britain's devaluation of the pound on Nov. 18, 1967, with an increase of the basic British interest rate to 8 per cent,

---

[19] See "Monetary Policy in Prosperity," *E.R.R.*, 1964 Vol. I, pp. 323-339.

the Federal Reserve Board raised the discount rate by one-half of a percentage point (to 4½ per cent) to present a massive outflow of dollars to England. American investments in Europe have created a "Eurodollar" market which lacks official status and is virtually free of governmental controls —American or foreign. Eurodollars are, in effect, "expatriate" American funds held by individuals, by American and European companies, and by foreign governments. Their total is estimated at between $25 billion and $30 billion.[20] Because there are no reserve requirements on Eurodollars, they are the most usable form of funds that big American commercial banks can obtain quickly to provide their customers with lendable funds during periods of credit-tightening at home. As long as these funds are available, the Fed's credit-tightening is not as effective as it might otherwise be.

Board member Andrew F. Brimmer issued figures in Paris on Feb. 11, 1969, showing a billion-dollar inflow to American commercial banks from their overseas branches during December and the first three weeks of January. Other, unofficial, estimates had put the inflow at $2.5 billion since Jan. 1. Even the larger figure would not compensate for time deposit losses of American banks in recent weeks. Commercial banks lost $3.5 billion in certificates of deposit between mid-December and early February, indicating that corporations were withdrawing their bank savings for higher-yield investments elsewhere or for their own cash needs. Banks are permitted to pay only 6½ per cent interest on "C.D.s"— deposits running to tens and hundreds of thousands of dollars.

LAG BETWEEN ACTION BY FED AND MARKET REACTION

Big banks have been resisting pressure from the Fed to cut back on their lending. One view is that they do not believe that the Fed—in spite of its strong words—is willing to make credit so tight that the economy will be pushed to the brink of a recession. Another view, often espoused by Federal Reserve officials, is that a lending cutback is not usually apparent at the beginning of a credit-tightening process. Banks will continue to make loans to favored business customers as long as their funds last—and these customers will continue borrowing unless they believe that interest rates will go even higher than they are now.

---

[20] See "American Investments in European Industry," *E.R.R.*, 1968 Vol. I, pp. 61-80.

There is also the view that the Federal Reserve's credit-control mechanism is not as effective as "Chicago school" monetary theorists and some others portray it. The *Economic Review* of the Cleveland Reserve Bank commented in its January 1969 issue that there was "wide agreement among economists on the large number of possible slippages between Federal Reserve actions and the behavior of the money supply." Edwin Dale made a similar point in the *New York Times* on Feb. 2, 1969:

> The Federal Reserve, it often seems, hurls thunderbolts and nothing happens. It raises the discount rate and it furiously buys and sells Treasury bills. It watches such arcane things as the federal funds rate and net borrowed reserves and the bank credit proxy. It tells the world that, by golly, it means business in stopping inflation. . . .
>
> And what happens? Everybody keeps on borrowing just as before. Banks and other lenders keep on lending pretty much as before. The money supply—for those who care about it—keeps on expanding. The Fed's own internal predictions of money and the like turn out to be frequently mistaken just as before.

Dale added: "The Fed may yet pull off a real slowdown in borrowing this time. Who knows? Not the Fed."

Economic forecasting, it is often suggested, is still more an art than a science—and forecasters at the Federal Reserve suffer no less from error than do their colleagues on the Joint Economic Committee of Congress and on the President's Council of Economic Advisers.[21] The ability to analyze an economic trend from volumes of confusing and sometimes contradictory statistics is only one part of the problem. The other is the lag between action by the Fed and reaction in the money markets. Measures taken to curb the late stages of a boom may achieve full effectiveness only in the recovery stage—when they will be harmful. Some economists hold that this is what happened in 1966, leading to the famous "credit crunch." The monetary theorists of Friedman's persuasion seize on that point to make their case for a fixed rate of expansion in the money supply.

---

[21] See "Economic Forecasting," *E.R.R.*, 1967 Vol. I, pp. 323-339. The federal budget for fiscal 1967 underestimated Viet Nam War costs in that year by $10 billion.

Future of U. S. Defense Economy

by

Park Teter

1 9 6 9
Sept. 24

FUTURE OF U. S. DEFENSE ECONOMY

DEFENSE SPENDING has been subjected in 1969 to more searching criticism than at any time since the cold war began. Attacks on the "military-industrial complex" in Congress and the press destroyed the nearly sacrosanct status formerly enjoyed by Defense Department budget requests. Although the critics failed to make any major dents in the military budget, the challenge they mounted was strong enough to put the Pentagon and its spokesmen in Congress on the defensive—a feat that would hardly have been possible a short while ago.

The outburst against military-industrial predominance coincided with four other developments pointing toward cutbacks in production for national defense: (1) The peace talks at Paris and initial troop withdrawals from Viet Nam focused attention on the economic consequences of bringing the war to an end; (2) plans for a multi-billion-dollar anti-ballistic missile system and other high-priced weapons sharpened interest in getting U. S.-Soviet talks on strategic arms limitation under way; (3) rising pressure for domestic programs to deal with the crisis in the cities established serious competition for dollars now spent on defense; and (4) inflation impelled the Nixon administration to effect certain cuts in the military budget. This multiple threat confronted defense industries, their employees, and their communities with the prospect of major dislocations in the foreseeable, if not the immediate, future.

REVOLT AGAINST MILITARY-INDUSTRIAL COMPLEX

When the Senate on Aug. 6 accepted development of the Safeguard A.B.M. system by a hairbreadth 50-50 vote, it was clear that the cold war tradition of congressional acquiescence in defense budgets was dead. The next day the Senate voted 47-46 to require quarterly Pentagon reports on all major weapons systems contracts and General Accounting Office audits and reports on such contracts. The military

143

procurement authorization bill was soon subjected to a blitz of proposed reductions.

Attacks on the A.B.M. were only one reflection of growing disenchantment with the defense establishment.[1] Supervision of military spending had been growing into a major issue as mounting public impatience with high taxes and inflation gave new weight to familiar charges of waste and war-profiteering in defense procurement. Such charges gained wide publicity during hearings in November 1968 and January 1969 before the Subcommittee on Economy of the Joint Economic Committee. In a report on May 27, 1969, the sub-committee, chaired by Sen. William Proxmire (D Wis.), said Pentagon procurement practices resulted in "a vast subsidy for the defense industry, particularly the larger contractors, and in a greatly inflated defense budget."

The *cause célèbre* of the hearings was the disclosure that the cost of the Lockheed Aircraft Corp.'s giant C-5A trans-port plane would run between $1.5 billion and $2 billion over the original contract estimate. The House and Senate Armed Services Committees held further hearings on the C-5A in May and June, and during September the aircraft was the key item in Senate debate on a $20 billion military procurement authorization. When it came to a showdown, Sept. 9, the Senate voted 64 to 23 against an amendment to limit Air Force purchases of the C-5A to 58 planes. An even larger majority, 75 to 7, voted Sept. 12 against an amend-ment to hold up construction of a $500 million nuclear air-craft carrier. And four days later, on Sept. 16, the Senate rejected 56-31 an amendment to slow down development of a new strategic bomber to replace the B-52.[2]

Although the revolt against military spending thus made no immediate headway in the Senate, and could not be ex-pected to fare differently in the House, it unquestionably represented a strong undercurrent of popular feeling that has shown no sign of abating. Public frustration over the Viet Nam war and its costs created a constituency for critics of military spending that demonstrated its strength in a Gallup poll reported Aug. 13, 1969. A majority of 52 per cent of the participants expressing an opinion said the United States was spending too much for national defense,

---

[1] See "Defense Criticism," *Congressional Quarterly Weekly Report,* March 28, 1969, pp. 451-453.

[2] For an earlier controversy on a successor to the B-52, see "Defense Spending Man-agement," *E.R.R.,* 1966 Vol. II, pp. 800-803.

31 per cent considered the rate of spending "about right," and 8 per cent favored increased defense expenditures.

The effect on the defense industry of the criticism in Congress and of public restlessness over military spending cannot be measured. But a recent article in *Fortune* magazine blamed "the changed political atmosphere" for the censure of the C-5A's cost and for hasty cancellation of an $875 million Lockheed contract for the Cheyenne helicopter.[3] The Defense Department's director of research and engineering, John S. Foster, conceded Aug. 19 that "Our past and present methods of acquiring weapons have lost us the confidence of the public." Foster warned that "the critical attitude toward the Defense Department may result in an actual reduction of the American effort" at a time when the Soviet Union is increasing military research and development.

TROOP WITHDRAWAL AND DEMOBILIZATION PLANNING

Although the Viet Nam peace talks drag on without apparent progress, pressure on the Nixon administration for a settlement and for large-scale U.S. troop withdrawals has not let up. Twenty-five thousand troops have already been pulled out, and an additional 35,000 are to be withdrawn by Dec. 15, 1969. On that date, however, the number of American troops remaining in Viet Nam may be as high as 484,000.

At the end of 1968 a special Cabinet committee submitted a report to President Johnson on economic planning for the period following the end of Viet Nam hostilities. The demobilization scenario on which the committee based its recommendations assumed full troop withdrawals would begin six months after a truce. In the following 12 months, total U.S. military personnel, at home and abroad, would be reduced by 800,000 and Defense Department civilian employees by 170,000 to produce an annual saving of $7 billion. Other operating expenditures would decline by $4 billion over a slightly longer period. After two and one-half years, military procurement would drop $8 billion below the level of spending required if the war were to continue.[4]

---

[3] Harold B. Meyers, "For Lockheed, Everything's Coming Up Unk-Unks," one of five articles on the defense industry in *Fortune*, Aug. 1, 1969.

[4] The committee's report was included in *Economic Report of the President* (January 1969), pp. 181-211. The total annual saving, two and one-half years after the truce, would fall $10 billion short of the estimated $29 billion a year being spent on the Viet Nam war. The difference arises from expected pay raises, price increases and program changes.

The President's 1969 Manpower Report estimated that about 900,000 of the 1.5 million civilians employed in defense-related jobs attributable to Viet Nam would be forced to seek new jobs. At the same time, reductions in the strength of the armed services would expand the civilian labor force.

Most economists stress the importance of maintaining a high level of demand in the economy as a whole as the most crucial factor in adjustment to sharp reductions in demand for defense production and services. Expansionary fiscal and monetary policies, however, may be limited by the continuation of U. S. balance-of-payments difficulties and threats to the international stability of the dollar.

INTENSIFICATION OF DEMAND FOR ARMS LIMITATION

While an end to the Viet Nam war is not likely to hurt the highly specialized industries producing strategic weapons, another possibility on the horizon is aimed directly at them. Strategic arms limitation talks (SALT) between the United States and the Soviet Union are expected to be launched soon—possibly as early as mid-October 1969. Past disarmament negotiations have done little to slow the arms race, but a number of factors now intensify the pressures for agreement:

(1) The cost of strategic weapons, especially when added to the cost of the Viet Nam war, has generated public pressure, particularly among new voters, for an arms agreement that would permit diversion of spending to domestic priorities. While less subject to public pressures, the Soviet Government also feels the pinch of imbalance in its economic development.

(2) Development of spy satellites and other intelligence devices simplifies policing of any agreement and reduces the need for on-site inspections, which have been a major obstacle to agreement.

(3) Technological changes, particularly development of A.B.M. and M.I.R.V. (multiple independently targeted re-entry vehicle) systems, place both countries on the threshold of a new and very costly phase of arms competition.

(4) The nuclear non-proliferation treaty, approved in the Senate on March 13, 1969, by an 83-15 vote, provides a recent precedent for U. S.-Soviet recognition of common peril in the arms race.

(5) The threat of Russian-Chinese hostilities puts pressure on Soviet leaders to seek a détente with the West and eases Western fears of a monolithic Eurasian Communist bloc.

(6) The Soviet Union's achievement of approximate military parity with the United States might make it more amenable to halting or reducing some types of arms production.[5]

[5] The Institute for Strategic Studies in London reported in April: "The Soviet Union must now be treated as a full equal [of the United States] in terms both of strategic power and of her ability to control conflict in the developing world."— Quoted in *Fortune*, Aug. 1, 1969, p. 85.

President Nixon's election campaign demand for American superiority rather than parity in arms was clarified at a Jan. 27 news conference when he abandoned both terms in favor of "sufficiency." [6]

Despite the urgency of arms limitation, precedent is all on the side of the skeptics. The much less complex nuclear test ban treaty of 1963 and this year's non-proliferation treaty each required more than four years of strenuous negotiation. Defense industry officials look for uninterrupted competition with Soviet weapons development, and they are not alone. An unidentified high official of the U. S. Arms Control and Disarmament Agency was recently quoted as saying:

> We are now at the edge of a precipice where we can escalate sharply. The industry thinks that agreements to limit arms are unlikely and will go all out to realize their expectations. We are at the threshold of another round in the arms race, just as we were eight years ago when we went all out for long-range missiles.[7]

Whatever happens to strategic weapons development, the forces it has been thought necessary to maintain against the contingency of local wars are likely to fall below pre-Viet Nam levels. Popular hostility toward future Viet Nams has already prompted the Senate to record its view, in a 70-16 vote on June 26, 1969, that overseas commitments must not be made without congressional approval. The Pentagon's assumption that the United States should be prepared to wage simultaneous wars in Europe and Asia, plus a smaller conflict elsewhere, is now being reconsidered in a major study of U. S. military posture under the direction of Deputy Defense Secretary David Packard.

CRIES TO STOP WAR AND TACKLE SOCIAL PROBLEMS

Ever since riots in the ghettos began to dramatize domestic problems in the United States, pressures have been building for increased attention to civilian priorities. Inevitably, those concerned about fighting poverty, pollution, crime, and racial prejudice, and improving education, health, and the urban environment looked jealously at the largest drain on federal funds—the defense budget. President Johnson's policies gave a double impetus to a basic shift in attitudes toward military expenditures. On the one hand, his Great

---

[6] See "Prospects for Arms Control," *E.R.R.*, 1969 Vol. I, pp. 276-277.

[7] Bernard D. Nossiter, "Arms Firms See Postwar Spurt," *Washington Post*, Dec. 8, 1968.

Society programs inspired hopes of solving long-standing social problems. On the other hand, the Viet Nam war took away the funds required for these programs.

By both discrediting global military efforts and hobbling social action at home, the war has contributed more than anything else to the current outcry against defense spending. The younger generation, who scarcely recall the cold war atmosphere of the Berlin airlift, the Korean War, or the "missile gap" but who are liable to be drafted to fight against the Viet Cong, are in the vanguard of the campaign to spend dollars on the underprivileged rather than on weapons. Pressures against defense spending may be expected to increase as this generation becomes an increasingly large portion of the electorate. In the 1970 elections the number of persons "under thirty" eligible to vote will number 4.7 million more than in the last off-year election of 1966 and will comprise 22.4 per cent of the voting-age population.

A list of new programs or major expansions of existing federal programs, included for purposes of illustration in President Johnson's 1969 Economic Report, bore a total estimated price tag of $40 billion for fiscal 1972. Assuming peace in Viet Nam, the funds expected to be available by then from reduced defense outlays plus natural growth in tax revenues were estimated to total only $22 billion.

The Nixon administration expects a smaller "peace and growth dividend." The size of this dividend has been the subject of much debate; it cannot be estimated with any confidence until the current review of global strategy and military posture is completed. Postponement of strategic weapons development during the Viet Nam war and expansion of the Soviet navy have generated strong demand in the Pentagon for costly new weapons.

Whatever the size of the dividend, its distribution may be largely determined before it even appears. President Nixon's welfare program, submitted to Congress Aug. 11, 1969, would add an estimated $4 billion to federal welfare costs in its first full year of operation. The President's plan for sharing federal revenues with the states would, if approved, take a growing chunk of the federal budget that would climb to about $5 billion by fiscal 1976. And if tax reforms expected this year take the form of the bill passed by the House

Aug. 8, revenue losses will reach $4.1 billion in calendar 1972. Administration plans to reduce the national debt, in order to make credit more readily available for private construction, would also reduce the amount available for other domestic programs. Another domestic priority—combating inflation—has already prompted the administration to cut $3 billion from the proposed fiscal 1970 defense budget.

Because projects for which the politicians and the public are impatient add up to so much more than peacetime budgets can finance, competition among them is certain to intensify jealousy of enormous defense expenditures. The domestic programs now under consideration could add to those ongoing obligations of the federal government which are extremely difficult to reduce and which have, in fact, a natural proclivity for expansion. The eventual result might be to reverse the present balance between defense and civilian spending, in which domestic programs have to fight for the scraps left by the military.

Economic Aspects of Military Spending

AS PRESIDENT Eisenhower observed in his farewell address, a permanent arms industry of vast proportions joined to an immense military establishment is "something new in the American experience." The way in which the economy adjusts, or fails to adjust, to major shifts in the defense industry will influence the course of the nation's adaptation to permanently threatened national security.

Despite the newness of its situation, the United States has had some experience with modern demobilization. There are lessons to be gained from those experiences, but there are also changes in the structure of the defense industry since the last major reduction in defense spending at the end of the Korean War.

Effects of Cutbacks After Big and Small Wars

During World War II there was grave concern that massive demobilization at the end of the war would plunge the nation back into the depression conditions of the 1930s. In the nine months following the war, almost eight million men were released from military service. An additional four million defense workers were laid off, thus freeing a total of 12 million or about one-fourth of the nation's work force. The postwar decline in defense spending was equivalent to one-third of the gross national product, an awesome amount when one considers that total defense spending now amounts to less than 10 per cent of the current G.N.P. And yet unemployment in the demobilization period after World War II never rose above 4 per cent.

The great success of the demobilization derived from high aggregate demand in the civilian sector. Postponed needs and pent-up consumer demand, accumulated during the war, kept the economy in high gear. The government helped the transition through tax reduction, veterans' benefits, rapid property disposal and contract terminations, and easy credit policies.

Though much smaller, the post-Korea demobilization caused a mild recession. Defense spending fell from $50.4 billion in fiscal 1953 to $40.7 billion in fiscal 1954, contributing to a rise in unemployment to 5.6 per cent of the labor force in 1954. Although tax cuts supported disposable income and consumption, economists feel that more vigorous fiscal and monetary policies would have eased the transition.[8]

Since the Korean War, other shifts in defense production have not caused severe dislocation. For example, a drop in spending for tanks, conventional ordnance and commercial types of hard goods from $11 billion in fiscal 1953 to about $2 billion in fiscal 1957 constituted a huge loss of defense business for the Midwest. But because the production and manpower resources involved were not highly specialized, they were readily diffused into a civilian economy sustained by high demand. During a leveling of defense spending in 1963-64, the national unemployment rate actually fell.

DIFFERENCES BETWEEN EARLIER WARS AND VIET NAM

Changes since the Korean War would affect the character of any adjustment to defense cutbacks today. In 1965 a special Presidential committee observed that earlier demobilizations largely entailed reconversion—a return to production of previously produced goods. Many of the manufacturers had assumed that defense work would be a temporary diver-

---

[8] See "Arms Cutbacks and Economic Dislocation," *E.R.R.*, 1964 Vol. I, p. 121.

sion. At present, numerous companies have never produced to any significant degree for non-military markets.[9]

This specialization is particularly evident in the highly scientific aerospace industry, which expanded rapidly following the Soviet Union's successful launching of its first satellite in 1957. However, during the Viet Nam war the aerospace industry's share of federal defense and space expenditures has fallen from a high of 30.7 per cent in fiscal 1964 to an estimated 25.7 per cent for fiscal 1970.[10]

The buildup for Viet Nam had its greatest impact on employment in the aircraft, ordnance and communications industries. In fiscal 1967, the latest for which figures are available, the jobs of about 100,000 additional workers in the ordnance industry were attributable to Viet Nam, and they accounted for 50 per cent of the employment in the industry generated by the Defense Department and to 37 per cent of total employment in the industry. The war added about 140,000 workers in the aircraft industry, and they constituted 30 per cent of defense-generated employment and 17.5 per cent of total employment in the industry. Around 50,000 additional workers in communications equipment production made up 22 per cent of the industry's defense-generated employment and about 7.5 per cent of its total employment.

In a number of industries large increases in employment due to Viet Nam constituted only a small portion of the total work force. For example, nearly two-thirds of defense-generated employment in clothing manufacture was derived from the buildup, but the more than 30,000 added workers made up only 2 per cent of total employment in the industry. Similar trends were evident in the manufacture of steel and nonferrous metals, chemicals and textiles.[11]

The spread of war production among industries with large civilian markets makes the current defense budget more like those of the Korean War and less like recent cold war emphasis on strategic weapons development and production. As a result, economist Murray L. Weidenbaum (now an Assistant Secretary of the Treasury) said two years ago:

[9] *Report of the Committee on the Economic Impact of Defense and Disarmament* (July 1965), p. 11.
[10] *1969 Aerospace Facts and Figures* (Aerospace Industries Assn.).
[11] Richard P. Oliver, "The Employment Effect of Defense Expenditures," *Monthly Labor Review*, September 1967, pp. 9-16. Slight revisions of figures given in the article are based on subsequent refinement of data by the Bureau of Labor Statistics. Updated figures are to be published in the December 1969 issue of the *Review*.

"Much of the expansion in Viet Nam requirements has been met by production of civilian-oriented industries which should experience relatively minor difficulties if aggregate demand is maintained in the economy as a whole. The companies and the localities which are most directly dependent on defense work might actually gain from a reorientation of the military budget away from conventional equipment and towards high technology products and services." [12]

REGIONAL IMPACT OF CURRENT DEFENSE SPENDING

The Viet Nam war has shifted somewhat the regional distribution of defense spending. The combined share of the three Pacific Coast states, while still larger than that of any other region, dropped from 24.7 per cent of the total dollar value of military prime contracts in fiscal 1965 to 19.1 per cent in fiscal 1968. The share of the South Central states in the same period rose from 10.4 to 16.7 per cent.

No other region shifted as much as two percentage points, but individual states experienced dramatic changes. Alabama, Connecticut, Illinois, Minnesota, Mississippi, Tennessee, Texas and Wisconsin in fiscal 1968 more than doubled their pre-war share of the dollar value of prime contracts. A few states experienced sharp reductions. Washington, for example, received $530 million in defense contracts in 1968, compared to $1.1 billion in fiscal 1964. Colorado in the same period dropped from $390 million to $263 million. [13]

Nine states in fiscal 1968 had over $200 in prime military contracts per inhabitant—California, Connecticut, Georgia, Indiana, Massachusetts, Missouri, New Hampshire, Texas and Vermont. It is often asserted that subcontracting spreads the spending more widely among the states, but a recent analysis of a sample of subcontracting employment figures cast some doubt on that hypothesis. [14]

Between June 1965 and June 1968 no state declined in employment attributable to defense. As one would expect, the largest absolute increases in defense-generated employment in this period occurred in more populous states—California (137,100), Texas (82,700), Pennsylvania (48,600)

[12] Murray L. Weidenbaum, *Peace in Vietnam: Possible Economic Impacts and the Business Response* (unpublished report prepared for the Committee on the Economic Impact of Peace in Vietnam, Chamber of Commerce of the United States, September 1967), p. 19.
[13] Murray L. Weidenbaum, "After Vietnam, Our Vietnamized Economy," *Saturday Review*, May 24, 1969.
[14] Roger F. Riefler and Paul B. Downing, "Regional Effect of Defense Effort on Employment," *Monthly Labor Review*, July 1968, pp. 1, 6.

Impact of Defense Spending, by States, 1965-1968

	Defense-generated employment (thousands)		Defense dependency ratio as % of labor force June '67	Military prime contracts fiscal '68 (millions)
	June '65	June '68		
Alabama	47.5	59.1	4.2	$ 409.2
Alaska	8.8	10.2	9.8	106.5
Arizona	14.9	26.1	4.2	287.1
Arkansas	5.6	11.5	1.7	121.3
California	354.4	491.5	6.5	6,471.9
Colorado	24.1	30.8	3.4	262.8
Connecticut	68.0	116.3	7.5	2,355.1
Delaware	2.0	2.8	1.3	42.6
District of Columbia	33.2	43.1	10.3	349.8
Florida	68.5	94.9	3.5	975.8
Georgia	58.4	77.2	4.8	964.2
Hawaii	20.8	27.7	8.8	95.6
Idaho	0.6	1.2	0.4	17.1
Illinois	48.7	83.3	1.8	932.1
Indiana	35.3	72.3	3.1	1,107.5
Iowa	7.9	13.8	1.2	261.0
Kansas	19.4	22.8	3.3	292.3
Kentucky	13.3	19.6	1.9	60.4
Louisiana	10.6	17.9	1.7	460.5
Maine	5.6	8.4	1.9	75.2
Maryland	70.7	87.5	6.9	703.5
Massachusetts	75.9	115.8	4.3	1,618.7
Michigan	30.3	39.3	1.4	796.3
Minnesota	17.3	34.6	2.2	620.3
Mississippi	23.3	38.0	3.1	369.2
Missouri	53.6	80.3	4.5	1,356.9
Montana	1.5	5.0	2.7	20.5
Nebraska	5.1	9.9	1.4	120.4
Nevada	3.0	3.3	1.6	17.9
New Hampshire	11.9	18.0	6.4	156.0
New Jersey	66.9	88.8	3.3	1,108.4
New Mexico	15.3	16.4	4.5	87.2
New York	132.2	168.4	2.1	3,483.7
North Carolina	26.0	44.3	2.0	487.3
North Dakota	2.7	5.6	1.3	68.1
Ohio	81.7	108.7	2.5	1,640.5
Oklahoma	31.0	43.6	4.4	164.9
Oregon	5.5	8.7	1.0	119.7
Pennsylvania	108.4	157.0	3.2	1,727.3
Rhode Island	13.4	17.1	5.3	126.4
South Carolina	19.2	28.0	3.0	133.0
South Dakota	2.1	2.7	0.7	33.6
Tennessee	25.0	45.8	2.8	541.6
Texas	118.1	200.8	4.3	4,087.2
Utah	28.7	36.2	9.9	131.2
Vermont	2.0	3.9	2.1	105.0
Virginia	112.6	149.7	8.4	692.7
Washington	45.7	54.5	4.3	529.6
West Virginia	4.9	8.6	1.5	132.0
Wisconsin	11.4	26.4	1.4	406.4
Wyoming	0.7	0.7	0.9	14.9
TOTAL	2,055.6	2,932.7	3.6	$37,248.1

and Connecticut (48,300). Excluding states with only very minor defense industry and installations, the sharpest *rate* of increase occurred in Indiana, Minnesota and Wisconsin, each of which at least doubled defense employment in the period.

These employment figures, compiled by the Economic Information System of the Defense Department and the National Aeronautics and Space Administration, reflected civilian employment in all military installations and in all prime contracts exceeding $10,000, but covered only the subcontracting reported by about 450 plants. The multiplier effect of defense employment on other production and services was not measured. The figures used indicated that defense employment absorbed more than 6 per cent of the work force in June 1967 in Alaska, California, Connecticut, the District of Columbia, Hawaii, Maryland, New Hampshire, Utah, and Virginia. The national average was 3.6 per cent.[15]

Means of Adjusting to Reduced Spending

CONFRONTED simultaneously by progressive withdrawal of American forces from Viet Nam, disarmament negotiations, attacks on the military-industrial complex, inflationary pressures on the defense budget, and a growing demand for domestic priorities, the defense industries face a troubled future. The fate of the companies engaged in defense production, of their employees, and of the communities in which they are situated will depend in large part on the adjustment of the national economy to reductions in military purchases. But even if the economy as a whole adjusts smoothly to defense cutbacks, there may be intense local difficulties. Advance planning for such difficulties is crucial to overcoming them.

AVAILABILITY OF VARIOUS TOOLS TO SUSTAIN DEMAND

The fiscal and monetary policies required to maintain aggregate demand during a decline in military demand will depend on the speed of demobilization and the trend of the economy at the time. In the scenario for Viet Nam peace outlined by President Johnson's special Cabinet committee

---

[15] See table on p. 721.

and included in the 1969 Economic Report, a shortfall of demand amounting to $18 billion, 18 months after a truce, was predicted in the absence of action to offset the drop in military expenditures.[16] Unless stabilizing action were taken, this gap could be multiplied by induced cutbacks in the private sector to reach $40 billion two years after the truce.

To maintain demand, the peace-and-growth dividend could be used either for increased government spending in civilian programs or for tax reductions that would stimulate private consumption. Some combination of these two approaches is generally expected. An end to the war-imposed income tax surcharge is a common feature of most projections, as is increased federal spending to reduce poverty and improve the urban environment.

Decisions on priorities among government programs and among tax cuts must depend in part on the pace of demobilization, because some policies stimulate demand more rapidly than others. Lead times in government programs, especially many federal grant programs to states and communities, delay their impact on purchases more than would be the case with tax reductions. Liberalization of such income-support programs as unemployment compensation or public assistance, and the acceleration of government expenditures already programed, are measures which would permit a more rapid stimulus than pursuit of new efforts. The 1969 Economic Report urged that a program of accelerated expenditures which could be instituted on short notice be available for the President's consideration. It estimated that such a program could add up to $3 billion to federal spending in six months, and up to $7.5 billion in 12 months. The report urged that any plans to be put into effect during a transition to peacetime spending be submitted to Congress soon for debate and perhaps for enactment on a standby basis.

Both government spending and tax cuts could be limited by the need for fiscal policies to combat inflation and improve the balance of international payments. Nixon administration officials have indicated that budget surpluses would be used after the Viet Nam war to reduce the national debt

---

[16] *Economic Report of the President* (January 1969), p. 195. Of the total shortfall, $16 billion would derive from reduced defense spending, and $2 billion would constitute the increment in demand needed to absorb the addition of 600,000 persons to the civilian labor force.

and thus make mortgage funds available at lower interest rates for private construction.

The Economic Report asserted that the basic choice between reducing taxes and increasing expenditures should not be governed by considerations of economic stabilization; various mixes of increased spending and reduced taxes would be equally satisfactory from that standpoint. The choice should depend, the report said, upon the extent to which the nation wishes to divert resources from defense uses into other areas of the public sector. It urged that priorities be set in advance.

Weidenbaum has warned that indecisiveness in monetary and fiscal responses to defense cutbacks, arising from hesitation in choosing among alternatives, might produce a needless recession. He has warned also that unemployment and fears of a major depression might result from inaction and in turn generate public pressure for large-scale government intervention and spending. "Were this to happen, the rapid expansion in the public sector brought about by the Viet Nam buildup might prove not to be temporary but to represent another long-term shift in the balance between public and private activities in the American economy." [17]

REEMPLOYMENT OF DEFENSE WORKERS AND VETERANS

In the rapid demobilization assumed in the Economic Report, there would be a net addition of 600,000 persons to the private labor force in the first 18 months after a Viet Nam truce. The decline in defense purchases would also require job shifts in the same period among as many as 750,000 additional workers. The two groups combined would be seeking an average of about 75,000 jobs per month above the normal rate. Because the monthly hiring rate in manufacturing alone averaged 730,000 in 1966 and 640,000 in 1967, the report regarded the post-Viet Nam employment needs as "significant—but not enormous."

A study, prepared for the U. S. Arms Control and Disarmament Agency, of the experiences of defense workers laid off at three aerospace defense plants, concluded that "The single most important reform of the labor market that would reduce appreciably the reemployment transition costs would be a sweeping overhaul of the [job] information channels." [18] The California Department of Employment, in

---

[18] *Reemployment Experiences of Defense Workers* (December 1968), p. iii.
[17] Murray L. Weidenbaum, *Peace in Vietnam: Possible Economic Impacts and the Business Response* (cited), p. 23.

a report likewise prepared for the Arms Control and Disarmament Agency, published information to facilitate job transfers from technical and skilled production occupations peculiar to the missile industry or so concentrated in that industry as to present transfer problems.[19] It found that most of the defense jobs it studied had counterparts in non-defense industries sufficiently similar in skills to permit transfer of workers with little or no additional training. Because missile production is among the most highly specialized defense industries, this finding augured well for reemployment in less sophisticated arms production. However, the California report noted that, even where skills were similar, in three out of four occupations surveyed the transfer to non-defense jobs was limited by at least one of the following factors: the demand for workers in the counterpart occupation, comparability of wages, union regulations, specific company hiring practices, and federal licensing requirements.

The California report emphasized the importance of the availability of information for reemployment; it specifically urged that the defense plant staff concerned with training or wages and salaries be fully utilized for its knowledge of similarities between defense and non-defense job requirements. The report proposed that defense contractors be required to classify all employee positions in accordance with the Dictionary of Occupational Titles in order to facilitate comparison of jobs from plant to plant.

PROGRAMS TO ASSIST WORKERS IN TRANSITION PERIOD

A number of federal programs already exist to aid workers caught in the transition to reduced defense efforts. Returning veterans receive particular attention from the federal-state Employment Service, and since 1967 special Veterans Assistance Centers have been established in 21 cities by the Veterans Administration. These centers place particular emphasis on the 25 per cent of veterans with less than a high school education. During their last six months in military service, men facing discharge without adequate work preparation are eligible for counseling, training, education and placement services provided at about 250 installations by a combination of private industry and federal, state and local agencies.

---

[19] California Department of Employment, *The Potential Transfer of Industrial Skills from Defense to Nondefense Industries* (April 1968), pp. 13-18.

The Department of Defense guarantees new job opportunities for career civilian employees dislocated by the closing of a military installation. The plan includes reimbursement for moving costs and protection of incomes during periods of transition. A computerized central referral unit in Dayton, Ohio, is used to match employees with vacancies. The program is not available to defense workers employed by private industry on government contracts.

Expansion of the federal-state Employment Service and training programs under the Manpower Development and Training Act would be required to handle increases in job seekers. The 1969 Economic Report recommended such expansion and also proposed a program of loans and grants for relocation assistance to low- and middle-income workers affected by cutbacks in specified defense-dependent communities. To prevent widespread loss of homes in areas suffering temporary unemployment, the report urged adoption of a program to encourage private lenders to defer mortgage payments on homes of persons dislocated by defense cutbacks. In the absence of such a moratorium, the report called for government loans to cover mortgage payments.

Whether or not unemployed defense workers should be singled out for more generous treatment than other unemployed persons has not been determined. The 1965 report of the President's Committee on the Economic Impact of Defense and Disarmament noted that a worker "bumped" by someone shifted from defense work, or a salesman laid off where retail trade had declined with defense production, was as deserving of assistance as an unemployed defense worker. The committee voiced doubt that relocation assistance would be justified except as part of a general program available to all.[20] Non-defense workers may well be the hardest hit. The 1969 Manpower Report observed that "A temporary rise in unemployment would intensify the job-seeking difficulties of disadvantaged workers with the flow into the labor market of educated, skilled and experienced workers competing for available jobs." [21]

The local adjustments to reductions in defense employment may have an important effect on the national economy.

---

[20] *Report of the Committee on the Economic Impact of Defense and Disarmament* (July 1965), p. 48.

[21] *Manpower Report of the President* (January 1969), p. 69.

Economist Leslie Fishman goes so far as to say that "micro" market adjustments may be decisive in maintaining employment because the balance-of-payments problem would inhibit fiscal policies that create demand in the national market. Fishman suggested that demobilization would offer an opportunity for "giant strides" in information channeling and employment decision theory that "could lead not only to smooth and successful transitions, but also to a new era in the operation of the labor markets." He asserted that "Improved operation of the labor market could easily reduce the unemployment rate to levels long familiar to the West German economy, increase efficiency and productivity, and thus become a strong force against inflation."[22]

PROGRAMS TO HELP DEFENSE-DEPENDENT COMMUNITIES

Although shifts in industrial production are a normal feature of the dynamic American economy, the volatile character of defense procurement makes communities which are heavily dependent on it subject to particularly severe dislocation.

The Defense Department's Office of Economic Adjustment since 1961 has sought to assist communities affected by closing of military installations. The office gives advice in analyzing a community's needs and assets and in planning for conversion and incorporation of obsolete installations into efforts organized by the community. It also provides liaison with federal agencies authorized to assist economic recovery. The office does not have legislative authority to assist communities affected by cutbacks in defense production by private industry.

However, a number of programs of civilian federal agencies are available to communities affected by major reductions in defense production. If unemployment suddenly rises to 50 per cent or more above the national average, or there is reason to expect it to reach that level, a community qualifies for assistance from the Economic Development Administration, established in the Commerce Department in 1965. Once the community has prepared an over-all economic development program, E.D.A. may provide any of the following: a) financial assistance for economic planning; b) technical assistance, research and informational aid; c) ad-

[22] Leslie Fishman, "Author's Note on Applicability to Economic Adjustment—Post Viet Nam and Disarmament," in *Reemployment Experiences of Defense Workers* (December 1968), pp. 230, 236.

vances for public works planning; d) plans to enable advance acquisition of land for public works; e) grants for public works; f) preferential treatment in disposal of surplus federal property; and g) loans to local development corporations.

Small Business Administration loans, Labor Department training programs, and grants to assist urban development planning also are available to communities adjusting to loss of defense activity. In communities affected by closing of government installations, the General Services Administration may ease the impact by arranging for use of the property by other federal agencies, by donating it for public purposes, or by selling it for industrial use.

Delay in implementing adjustment plans is likely to start a downward spiral in a community deprived of defense activity. As the work force scatters in search of jobs, it becomes more difficult to attract new enterprises. A consistent theme of studies of areas hit by defense cutbacks is the need for a local committee to develop in advance plans for community adjustment. Most studies stress that local initiative and responsibility are essential.

President Johnson's final Economic Report recommended establishment of a Readjustment Operations Committee for detailed planning of readjustment assistance and for coordination with state and local authorities. The proposed committee would also develop inventories of the skills of defense workers and military personnel for matching with the requirements of potential sources of employment in defense-dependent areas.

CONVERSION PROBLEMS OF THE DEFENSE CONTRACTORS

A corporation can cope with cuts in defense orders in three ways. It can sell or deactivate plant or equipment and continue to operate on a smaller scale while its manpower is diffused in the economy. It can diversify by developing or acquiring capacity to produce for civilian markets, in order to cushion the shock of defense cuts and pave the way for expansion in non-defense production. Or it can convert its entire productive capacity from swords to plowshares.

For many industries whose defense orders have expanded during the Viet Nam war, conversion would merely constitute a return to pre-war activities. To shift from production of items like uniforms and C-rations to civilian goods would require minimum adaptation. Companies for which military procurement provides only a small part of the total market, as in the case of automobile manufacturers, are sufficiently diversified to accommodate readily to defense cuts and shift resources to other activities.

A bill introduced in the House by Rep. F. Bradford Morse (R Mass.) and a companion bill in the Senate by Sen. George McGovern (D S.D.) would, in addition to creating a National Economic Conversion Commission, require all Defense Department and Atomic Energy Commission contractors to define their capability for converting their manpower and facilities from military to civilian uses.[23] The difficulties of such conversion were summarized in a recent study prepared for the U. S. Arms Control and Disarmament Agency by the University of Denver Research Institute:

> Unfortunately there is little evidence that defense firms can easily achieve rapid, profitable conversion. Defense industry is uniquely specialized. It is set up to develop and produce limited numbers of technically sophisticated, expensive systems. It is also organized to deal largely with a single, rich, hierarchically organized customer who participates actively in the management of each firm. Rapid conversion of defense industry resources appears feasible only when directed into fields with similar customer requirements and customer participation.[24]

Not all assessments have been so cautious. The very sophistication of such specialized industries as missile production tempts speculation on the benefits to be reaped by application of such concentrated talent to civilian problems. "The application of systems management techniques to a large variety of non-defense management and design problems holds great promise for the future," the 1965 report of the Economic Impact committee suggested.[25] The June 5, 1967, issue of *Technology Week* was devoted entirely to the market for aerospace capacities in federal agencies other than the Defense Department and NASA. It found prospective markets worth about $5 billion, including projects in fields as diverse as oceanology, high-speed ground transportation, and water pollution.

---

[23] The McGovern bill has a score of co-sponsors, and around 80 House members have introduced bills paralleling the Morse bill.

[24] University of Denver Research Institute, *Defense Systems Resources in the Civil Sector: An Evolving Approach, an Uncertain Market* (July 1967), p. 104.

[25] Report of the Committee on the Economic Impact of Defense and Disarmament (July 1965), p. 23.

ECONOMIC CONTROLS

by

Hoyt Gimlin

1 9 6 9
Aug. 13

ECONOMIC CONTROLS

TALK among economists is turning to the possibility that the federal government will have to invoke wartime controls over wages, prices, rents, bank lending and so on. The talk is stimulated by the inability of monetary and fiscal restraints thus far in 1969 to halt the nation's worst inflation in two decades. "If by the year-end the inflationary spiral shows no sign of responding to general monetary-fiscal restraint," the monthly *Economic Letter* of the Cleveland Central National Bank observed in June, "new approaches will have to be considered, and direct controls is one method that has worked in the past."

A Gallup Poll published in early July indicated that the American public was inclined to favor a freeze on prices and wages and to oppose an extension of the 10 per cent surcharge on federal income taxes.[1] Economist Robert Lekachman commented that "The public . . . may have a better grasp of the necessities of national economic policy than do the professional economists, who are perhaps too bedazzled by the beauties of free markets to notice how little of the economy matches their ideal." [2]

But in government, only Treasury Secretary David M. Kennedy has publicly suggested that direct controls over the economy might be forthcoming. President Nixon has specifically and strongly rejected the notion. "The Administration has ruled out wage and price controls as a way of dealing with inflation under conditions that are now foreseeable," a White House press statement said on July 16. Presidential press secretary Ronald L. Ziegler added that Nixon was "not for controls" and had "consistently taken this position." It was recalled that Nixon served for eight months in 1942 as a

---

[1] Of those responding to the poll, 47 per cent thought a price-wage freeze a "good idea" and 41 per cent thought it a "poor idea." The remainder had no opinion. On the surcharge, 38 per cent said it should be extended and 51 per cent opposed its extension.

[2] Robert Lekachman, "The Economy: Controls—Chapter Two," *Dun's Review*, June 1969, p. 13.

lawyer in the Office for Emergency Management[3]—an experience that is known to have instilled in him a strong distaste for the complex and sometimes cumbersome economic control machinery.

The White House statement did not still the growing debate over whether controls are needed, nor did it seem to foreclose the possibility that in time the President might change his mind. Nixon had told a news conference on June 19 that "we will have to look to other courses of action" if decisions to cut the federal budget, tighten credit and extend the surtax do not "begin to have some effect within two or three months." The President did not say what new action was contemplated, but it was recalled elsewhere that Secretary Kennedy had said—and was to repeat later—that wage and price controls were among the measures the administration would consider.

Kennedy, testifying before the House Banking and Currency Committee on June 30, 1969, said that he personally did not favor direct governmental controls over the economy to check inflation, but added that "We may have to resort to them if current efforts do not succeed." On the previous day the President's Economic Counselor, Arthur F. Burns, denied that such controls were being considered. "Then there will be no controls?" Burns was asked on the ABC-TV "Issues and Answers" program. "I say that flatly," he answered. Further denials were made by Commerce Secretary Maurice H. Stans. It was amid the resulting confusion of conflicting views from within the administration that the White House statement of July 16 was issued.

ECONOMY'S DEFIANCE OF FISCAL-MONETARY CURBS

Washington officials do not disguise their dismay over the economy's continued defiance of their efforts to slow it down by indirect means. The surtax was levied in mid-1968 for one year and then extended for six months, through 1969, as an anti-inflationary measure. The Federal Reserve System began imposing monetary restraints in earnest in December 1968, and since then bank credit has shrunk,[4] driving interest rates to record and near-record heights. Major big-city banks

---

[3] O.E.M., now defunct, was the framework agency for a host of civilian offices involved in administering economic controls in World War II, including the Office of Price Administration.

[4] As measured by the total reserves of member banks in the Federal Reserve System. In the second quarter of 1969, the latest reported, these reserves decreased at a 9 per cent annual rate. See "Money Supply in Inflation," *E.R.R.*, 1969 Vol. I, pp. 145-161.

on June 10, 1969, raised their "prime" rate on lending to favored business customers for the fourth time in six months, to an all-time high of 8½ per cent. The federal budget, too, took an anti-inflationary turn when spending cuts in fiscal 1969, combined with larger-than-expected receipts, produced a $3.07 billion surplus—the first budget surplus in nine years.

However, the Consumer Price Index, the most widely used measurement of inflation, remained oblivious to these events. It recorded a 5.5 per cent rise in the cost of living in the 12 months from July 1968 through June 1969. By contrast, 24 months elapsed before the index climbed 5.5 per cent above the point where it stood when the present inflationary movement was first detected in the early months of 1965. In other words, inflation has been advancing recently at twice as fast a pace as in the beginning. And the 3.2 per cent rise in consumer prices recorded in the first six months of 1969 threatens to make this the country's worst year of inflation since 1947, when the index jumped 9.1 per cent.

In theory, a combination of tight bank credit, higher taxes and reduced federal spending will lead to a cut in industrial production, which will lead in turn to a loss of jobs, income and purchasing power. This progression is supposed finally to lower the pressure on prices. According to current economic thinking, there is a lag of six months or so before prices respond to such treatment. By that reckoning, some signs of response should become visible soon. But by August 1969 the economic indicators were continuing to give a muddled picture. The economy as measured in terms of the Gross National Product did show a slowdown in "real" growth in 1969—growth after the inflation factor was subtracted. But no corresponding slowdown could be detected in jobs, income or prices. "Despite continuing signs of some moderation," the *Monthly Review* of the New York Federal Reserve Bank observed in July, "the economy remains vigorous and inflationary expectations are still strong."

STEEL PRICE INCREASES AND RISING LABOR COSTS

There is growing concern that the wage-price spiral will be pushed even higher by new steel price increases and by a new round of labor demands in the offing. The United States Steel Corp., bellwether of the industry, announced July 30, 1969, an average price increase of 4.8 per cent on steel used to make automobiles, refrigerators and many other consumer products. It was the broadest steel price increase since July 31, 1968, when Bethlehem Steel Corp. announced a 5 per cent increase, which it halved a few days later under pressure from the Johnson administration.

In making its announcement, U. S. Steel noted that wage increases effective Aug. 1 under an existing contract with the United Steelworkers of America would add substantially to the production cost of its products. The corporation had reported a decline in profits during the April-June quarter, which it attributed in part to rising labor costs. The Bureau of Labor Statistics reported that gross weekly earnings of workers in private industry reached a record $115.06 in June 1969, a gain of $1.58 over the previous month. But the workers had about one-half of one per cent less spendable income than they did a year earlier because of higher taxes and inflation.

"In many executive suites," the *Wall Street Journal* commented July 14, 1969, "it has been fashionable for at least a year to depict the inflationary spiral as a clear case of sharply rising labor costs pushing up prices. This may or may not be right. . . . Whatever the truth, it's increasingly apparent that rising labor costs are likely to play the major role in U. S. inflation from now on. A major reason is simply that organized labor, understandably chagrined by inroads that inflation and taxes have made into past pay gains, seems in no mood to settle for modest increases in new contracts."

Contracts for seven million workers in several major industries expire within 18 months, beginning in the autumn with the electrical union employees at General Electric and Westinghouse. Economic columnist Joseph R. Slevin has reported that "Union leaders are setting their sights on record-smashing 10 per cent boosts." [5]

Secretary of Labor George P. Shultz told a news conference July 25 that under labor agreements concluded during the first six months of 1969 the median wage-benefit increase amounted to 7.1 per cent annually, and that increases in the construction trades averaged 15 per cent. "I'm not going to tell them what to agree to," Shultz said in response to a question, "although I admit I have my reservations about these 15 per cent increases." His comment was about the

---

[5] *Washington Post,* July 6, 1969.

closest that anyone in the Nixon administration had come to suggesting guidelines for wage or price increases. The President said at his first White House news conference, Jan. 27, that "I do not go along with the suggestion that inflation can be effectively controlled by exhorting labor and management and industry to follow certain guidelines." He added that "The primary responsibility for controlling inflation rests with the national administration and its handling of fiscal and monetary matters."

ROOT CAUSES OF DIFFERENT KINDS OF INFLATION

Aside from political ideology, the current dispute over how to deal with inflation seems to stem from disagreement over what is causing it. The word "inflation" is sometimes used to describe both higher prices and their causes. It may refer to an expansion of the money supply and credit in excess of the supply of goods (monetary inflation) ; large deficits in the federal budget (fiscal inflation) ; an increase in prices out of proportion to an increase in costs (profits inflation) ; and an excess of labor costs over gains in productivity (wage inflation).

The first two forms of inflation (monetary and fiscal) generate what economists describe as *demand-pull* pressures, which come from too much money chasing too few goods. Profits and wage inflation contribute to *cost-push* pressures. The Nixon administration and the semi-independent Federal Reserve Board tend to see the current inflation as largely of the demand-pull variety. But the Johnson administration centered a large part of its anti-inflation effort on cost-pull pressures. It tried to keep price and wage increases within explicit guidelines (or "guideposts"). During Johnson's final weeks in office his Cabinet Committee on Price Stability issued a staff study which attributed much of the inflationary surge to powerful labor unions and monopolistic business enterprises.

"Large profits may serve as enticing targets," the study stated. "When trade unions seek to share these profits by demanding wage gains exceeding the rate of increase in over-all productivity, firms with market power may protect their excess profits by either passing forward the higher labor costs or failing to reduce prices." [6] The after-tax profits

---

[6] *Studies by the Staff of the Cabinet Committee on Price Stability* (January 1969), p. 41. Members of the committee were Joseph W. Barr, Treasury Secretary; C. R. Smith, Commerce Secretary; W. Willard Wirtz, Labor Secretary; Charles W. Zwick, Budget Director; and Arthur M. Okun, chairman, Council of Economic Advisers.

of manufacturing corporations in 1968 averaged 12 per cent; in the same period, labor costs per unit of production in private industry as a whole increased 4.6 per cent—matching almost precisely the advance in the Consumer Price Index.

Perhaps the majority view in government at present is that there may be multiple causes of inflation, but that inflation can nevertheless be brought under control by use of the traditional remedies of tight money and spending cuts—if the public will only be patient long enough. But impatience is manifest everywhere. Members of Congress report that their mail is heavy with letters from constituents protesting the steadily rising cost of living, especially higher food prices.

Eliot Janeway, financial writer, contends that consumers who want price controls and employers who want wage controls "are not putting on enough pressure to force either; and each set of voices is neutralizing the other." But he adds that mayors and governors, who have political muscle, will soon be forced to demand direct controls over bank credit so that municipalities and states can sell their bonds on the market at interest rates they can afford to pay. "State and local governments," he wrote recently, "have long since exhausted their bank balances; anticipated tax receipts; tapped their banks dry of lending power; and are now running their contractors and suppliers out of money." [7]

The Janeway proposal would entail an expansion of the nation's money supply by the Federal Reserve System,[8] followed by the imposition of controls that would give public agencies rather than private business priority among borrowers. Gov. Marvin Mandel of Maryland expressed a similar thought to the House Banking and Currency Committee, June 22, 1969: "If the federal government is going to use interest rates to control inflation, then we're going to have to find some way to ration money." He complained that his state's building program was being crippled by high interest rates.

The Federal Reserve, however, has strongly opposed any suggestion that it impose credit rationing or similar direct controls upon commercial banks. Appearing before the same congressional committee on June 30, Federal Reserve Chairman William McChesney Martin Jr. rejected also the idea of

---

[7] *The Janeway Service* newsletter, July 2, 1969, p. 3.
[8] See "Money Supply in Inflation," *E.R.R.*, 1969 Vol. I, pp. 145-161.

a voluntary system of credit allocation. He said that "Voluntary programs run the risk of penalizing those who cooperate, if their competitors cooperate less fully." Beginning in 1965, American banks subscribed to voluntary controls on investments in an effort to improve this country's international balance of payments. Martin testified that the Voluntary Foreign Restraint Program involved only a few large banks, and he asserted that the same effectiveness could not be attained under a domestic program involving all of the country's 13,000 commercial banks.

Direct Economic Controls in Past Wars

THE GOVERNMENT has ample precedent for imposing direct controls on the American economy in wartime. Key areas of the economy came under detailed government supervision in World Wars I and II and in the Korean conflict.[9] Soon after America's entry into World War I, President Wilson ordered price controls placed on a wide range of commodities, under authority derived from acts of Congress and from his war powers as commander in chief. Controls in World War II were even more extensive, extending to wages, rents, and rationing. During the Korean War, controls were invoked again but on a smaller scale than in World War II. In each of the three wars the controls were controversial, hard to administer and not entirely effective. However, it is the consensus of economists that imposition of direct controls on those occasions was instrumental in holding back inflation.

PRICE-FIXING METHODS EMPLOYED IN WORLD WAR I

Price controls began in World War I on Aug. 21, 1917, four and one-half months after the United States declared war on Germany. On that date, a schedule of maximum prices for the sale of bituminous coal at the mine was proclaimed. Two days later, a similar schedule for anthracite coal was proclaimed, and on Aug. 30 a "fair price" for wheat was announced. From then until the end of the war, price controls were gradually extended. In September 1917, only

---

[9] See "Experiments in Price Controls," *E.R.R.*, 1937 Vol. I, pp. 431-449; "Enforcement of Price and Rent Controls," *E.R.R.*, 1951 Vol. I, pp. 299-314; and "War Powers of the President," *E.R.R.*, 1966 Vol. I, pp. 183-199.

50 of the 1,366 commodities listed on the wholesale price index were subject to price control; by November 1918, the last month of the war, 573 were controlled.

The Food and Fuel Control Act of Aug. 10, 1917, granted President Wilson authority to set up the Food Administration and the Fuel Administration. Prices of most basic raw materials other than food and fuel were administered initially by the War Industries Board and after March 14, 1918, by the Price-Fixing Committee. The raw materials included iron and steel, cotton textiles, building materials, acids and a variety of other items. The War Trade Board, created by the President under powers granted by the Espionage Act and the Trading With the Enemy Act, had control over imports and exports. It used its licensing powers to impose—indirectly—price levels on imported goods. The War and Navy departments used their requisitioning and commandeering powers to some extent to control prices of their own purchases.

Government authorities thought it necessary to let prices rise enough to encourage production adequate to meet the extraordinary wartime needs. Controls were intended to keep prices from going beyond that point. Except for a few commodities, the government did not attempt to fix the specific price at which goods were to be sold. Controls usually took the form of maximum prices and maximum margins of profit; prices might fluctuate freely below those ceilings. In practice, however, maximum prices almost invariably became the actual prices and in effect amounted to fixed prices.

Enforcement of food prices was achieved mainly through an elaborate licensing system which Congress authorized in the Food and Fuel Control Act. Persons engaged in importing, manufacturing, storing, mining or distributing food products were required to be licensed and to abide by licensing regulations. Only retailers with gross annual sales below $100,000 and farm producers were exempt. By the end of the war 263,737 firms, individuals and corporations had been licensed by the Food Administration.

The War Industries Board and the Price-Fixing Committee, in contrast, had little direct power to set prices. But recalcitrant industries could be threatened with the loss of priorities for raw materials or transportation if they balked at suggested price levels.

In April 1917, the month the United States entered the war, the wholesale price index rose 14 points to a new high of 170 (in terms of the 1913-14 base level of 100). In July, shortly before the first controls were imposed, the index stood at 189; by the war's end it had risen only to 200. The effectiveness of wartime price controls can be judged in another way. Beginning in the autumn of 1916, the wholesale index numbers for the group of commodities later to be placed under price controls started rising faster than the index numbers for commodities that would remain uncontrolled throughout the war. But by November 1918, the two sets of commodities—controlled and uncontrolled—showed precisely the same index figures.

Price controls were lifted soon after the Armistice, and prices rose rapidly during the following winter and spring. A newly created Industrial Board tried to halt inflation by persuading producers and distributors to establish "fair prices." But the project foundered and in May 1918 all the board members resigned. At President Wilson's request, Congress in 1919 renewed anti-profiteering provisions of the lapsed Food and Fuel Control Act and appropriated $1 million to enforce them. Attorney General A. Mitchell Palmer revived the wartime system of fair-price committees under state food administrators and charged them with determining whether retail prices were excessive. Some 1,600 companies and persons were indicted, and 181 were convicted of profiteering. Prices began to turn down in the summer of 1920, but the decline was attributed less to the government's campaign than to an extensive buyers' strike. Consumers were showing a strong determination to stay away from stores until prices dropped.

PRICE, WAGE AND OTHER CONTROLS IN SECOND WAR

Voluntary price controls preceded America's entry into World War II. The Price Stabilization Division of the National Defense Advisory Commission was created in 1940 as an element of a war preparedness program. President Roosevelt declared that the United States, though officially neutral, would become the "arsenal of democracy"—words that conveyed the idea of furnishing arms but not troops to the Allies. Leon Henderson, as head of the Price Stabilization Division and of its successor, the Office of Price Administration, worked with some success to win industry's cooperation in holding down prices of materials for defense production.

Mandatory price controls were not instituted until after Pearl Harbor. The Price Control Act of Jan. 30, 1942, provided the legal foundation for a network of price controls, but it specified that "Nothing in this act shall be construed to authorize the regulation of compensation paid by the employer to any of his employees." Despite that stricture against wage controls, the National War Labor Board on July 16, 1942, issued its famous "Little Steel formula." The board, which had been set up by executive order to arbitrate wartime labor disputes, held in this case that workers at the four "Little Steel" companies [10] were due a 15 per cent cost-of-living raise.

An executive order issued Oct. 3, 1942, under the Price Stabilization Act signed the previous day, instructed the War Labor Board not to "approve any increases in wage rates prevailing on Sept. 15, 1942, unless such increase is necessary to correct maladjustment or inequities, to eliminate substandards of living, to correct gross inequities, or to aid in the effective prosecution of the war." The order, in effect, applied the Little Steel formula to all industry.

Consumer credit controls had been established by executive order in 1941 to discourage excessive buying at a time when more money was available than civilian goods. The size of down payments was raised and the time for payment of installment purchases was shortened. These controls covered a variety of commodities and were administered by the Federal Reserve Board. Most of them remained in effect until late 1946, more than a year after the war's end. Some were briefly reinstated in 1948 because of postwar inflation but soon lapsed again as prices began to ease. William McChesney Martin Jr. told Congress in mid-1969 that the Federal Reserve would again like to have standby authority to impose similar credit controls on credit purchases.

RESULTS OF EARLY POSTWAR LIFTING OF CONTROLS

In the early months of 1946 it became apparent that the nation was on the verge of serious inflation despite a sharp reduction in federal spending as the nation converted from a wartime to a peacetime economy. President Truman in his State of the Union message that year asked Congress to extend controls on prices and rents beyond their June 30

---

[10] Bethlehem Steel Corp., Republic Steel Corp., Youngstown Sheet and Tube Co., and Inland Steel Co. See "Revision of the Little Steel Formula," *E.R.R.*, 1944 Vol. II, pp. 135-149.

expiration date. Almost all other direct wartime economic controls, except on consumer credit, had been removed or reduced by the end of 1945.

Congress responded by extending for one year the life of the Office of Price Administration; however, it specified that the main function of the agency would be to decontrol rents and all prices except the prices of sugar and rice. Congress sensed that the nation was weary of wartime controls and was in no mood to keep them. During debate in 1946, Rep. Dudley G. Roe (D Md.) argued that the sooner "we get rid of the O.P.A. and let God's laws function without human interference, the sooner we will have peace and prosperity." [11]

Truman's warning in January 1946 that "inflation is our greatest immediate domestic crisis" was soon borne out. The Consumer Price Index went up 18.1 per cent that year, a rise which to date has been exceeded only once—by a 20 per cent increase in 1918.[12] The rate of the "galloping" inflation of 1946 was halved in 1947 and slowed to a "creeping" 1.2 per cent inflation in 1948.

Toward the end of the war, the question of full employment had become uppermost in the minds of many Americans. The sweeping reduction of government expenditures, expected in the wake of conversion to a peacetime economy, raised specters of the massive unemployment suffered in the Great Depression and occasioned extensive consideration of means to create new civilian jobs. The declared purpose of a proposed "Full Employment Act of 1945" was to assure "a useful and remunerative job" to everyone able and anxious to work.[13] The Employment Act finally put on the statute books in 1946 had the more modest goal of promoting "maximum employment, production and purchasing power." By that time, release of the long pent-up consumer demand for all kinds of goods had dispelled the earlier fears of postwar unemployment and produced an inflationary situation. The government's commitment to promote full employment remained, however, and has been the cornerstone of economic policy to the present day. It is a commitment which often has been hard to reconcile with attempts to maintain price stability.

---

[11] *Congress and the Nation 1945-64* (publication of Congressional Quarterly, 1945), p. 347.

[12] 1913 is the earliest year for which the figures have been compiled.

[13] See "Full Employment," *E.R.R.*, 1945 Vol. II, pp. 61-78.

The outbreak of war in Korea in June 1950 precipitated a new round of inflation and a revival of economic controls. Hoarders scrambled for goods in the expectation of scarcities and sent prices soaring; the wholesale price index advanced 12 per cent from June to December. President Truman asked Congress on July 19 for authority to freeze wages and prices and to invoke a wide set of other controls.

PRICE, WAGE AND MONEY POLICIES IN KOREAN WAR

The Senate Republican leader, Robert A. Taft of Ohio, said that the program, if adopted, "probably means an end to economic freedom in the United States, perhaps forever." But complaints from constituents about rising prices, together with the testimony of Bernard M. Baruch, a dominant figure in mobilization for the two World Wars, persuaded Congress to grant some of Truman's requests. The Defense Production Act of 1950, as signed into law Sept. 8, authorized the President to assign priorities, allocate materials and facilities, and requisition property for defense production; to regulate consumer credit and credit on new real estate construction; and to impose selective or general price controls.

Controls of consumer credit were reimposed Sept. 18 and tightened a month later. The newly created Economic Stabilization Agency, unable to persuade automobile makers to rescind price increases voluntarily, in mid-December ordered them to do so, the first time selective price controls were used in the Korean war. The Office of Price Stabilization followed on Jan. 26, 1951, by issuing a "General Ceiling Price Regulation" which froze the prices of most goods and services by fixing each seller's ceiling at the highest price at which the product was offered or delivered during the period between Dec. 19 and Jan. 25. There was no price rollback.

The regulation applied in general at all levels—retail, wholesale, and manufacturing. Exclusions included prices of newspapers and magazines, professional fees, public utility rates, and farm commodities selling below parity as determined by the Secretary of Agriculture. General Wage Stabilization Regulation 1, issued at the same time by the Wage Stabilization Board, prohibited payment or receipt of wages, salaries or other compensation at rates higher than those in effect Jan. 25, without prior approval by the board.

Inequities in the price structure were eased by a series of "tailored" regulations. By the end of September 1951, there were 63 regulations of this kind, applying, for example, to retailers of apparel, to wholesalers and retailers of food, and to manufacturers of consumer durables. To permit adjustments in the wage pattern that existed at the time of the freeze, the Wage Stabilization Board authorized increases up to 10 per cent beyond the January 1950 levels. Moreover, in August 1951, cost-of-living adjustments were authorized for all workers.

The wholesale price index leveled off in February 1951 after a rapid 15-point increase during the second half of 1950. Consumer prices, slower to decline, showed a 5.9 per cent gain in 1951 but a gain of less than one per cent the following year. Monetary policy helped to dampen inflationary pressures perhaps as much as controls during the Korean War—in contrast to the situation in World War II.

The Treasury realized in World War II that it would need to borrow large sums from the banking system to finance the war effort. Treasury officials believed it was essential that interest rates, especially on government securities, be kept low. In response to this need, the Federal Reserve System obligated itself to buy all securities offered by commercial banks. Thus when a commercial bank needed additional reserves to support heavier loan demands that arose in a booming wartime economy, it would sell a portion of its government securities. These sales had the effect of expanding the money supply and made inflation harder to control.[14] The Treasury-Federal Reserve arrangement came to an end in March 1951, and as the "Fed" regained a degree of control over the size of the money supply, it could aid in the fight against inflation.

Control programs in the Korean War were smaller than in World War II, but they again generated controversy.[15] Several congressional committees held extended hearings on profiteering in "gray markets" for scarce goods and others investigated "influence peddling." Organized labor withdrew its representation from the Office of Defense Mobilization

---

[14] See "Federal Budget Making," *E.R.R.*, 1969 Vol. I, pp. 3-19, and "National Debt Management," *E.R.R.*, 1967 Vol. II, pp. 885-902.

[15] The Office of Price Administration alone employed about 80,000 persons in World War II; only about 17,000 persons worked for control agencies during the Korean War, about 12,000 in the Office of Price Stabilization.

early in 1951 in protest against its "big business domination." Charles E. Wilson of General Electric was in charge of O.D.M.

The Eisenhower administration, taking office in January 1953, did not ask Congress to renew authority for price-wage controls, and by the end of March almost all of them were dismantled. President Eisenhower in his first State of the Union address described the controls as "largely unsatisfactory and unworkable." Consumer prices showed no perceptible rise in the months after controls were lifted—a fact which led critics to say that prices had been set too high originally.

Wage-Price Guideposts and Alternatives

THE DEMISE of direct controls over wages and prices in 1953 did not signal a hands-off policy by government. President Eisenhower, like President Truman before him, occasionally exhorted business and labor to use restraint. This "jawbone policy" was used forcefully and specifically by Presidents Kennedy and Johnson to keep wages and prices within fixed guidelines—or guideposts—which their administrations devised.

The idea of guideposts preceded the 1960s. Economists had argued for some time that something was wrong with the classical explanation of general price inflation—monetary demands for goods exceeding the economy's ability to produce them. This theory failed to explain a general rise in prices which occurred in the years 1955-1958 when there was unused productive capacity. The search for an explanation led to the concept of cost-push inflation: the ability of powerful labor unions to raise wages or of monopolistic business enterprises to raise prices.[16]

President Kennedy made guidepost policy explicit in his *Economic Report* to Congress in January 1962. His guidepost proposals, while filled with complexities, contained two

---

[16] A broader theoretical basis for the guideposts is the concept of *demand-shift* inflation, put forth by the Joint Economic Committee of Congress in 1959 in its *Study of Employment, Growth and Price Levels*. According to that concept, shifting demands within the economy may produce wage-price increases in one sector without offsetting reductions in another.

central features: (1) average wage increases should keep pace with average increases in productivity for the economy as a whole, and (2) price changes should reflect changes in productivity so that, for example, prices would decline in industries where productivity advanced more rapidly than the average for the economy.

Two years later, President Johnson and his economic advisers stated the guideposts in terms of a numerical formula —that wage or price increases exceeding 3.2 per cent a year were inflationary. The government reasoned that the formula, if readily understood, would draw public support. But there were complaints from unions and management that needed flexibility was being sacrificed to public understanding.

Kennedy and Johnson both sought to mobilize public opinion behind their efforts to make guidepost policy stick. Kennedy's celebrated encounter with the U. S. Steel Corp. in April 1962 came three months after the policy was announced. Steel was a highly "visible" industry and its prices affected many others—in automobiles, construction, home appliances and the like. The government feared that an inflationary settlement between U. S. Steel and the steelworkers' union might set off a wage-price spiral, stunt the nation's economic growth, keep unemployment high, weaken the dollar abroad, and damage the U. S. balance of international payments.

Under pressure from Washington, the union agreed March 31, 1962, to accept a small increase in fringe benefits and to forgo a wage increase. When the arrangement was made public, Kennedy described it as "non-inflationary" and praised the two parties for "industrial statesmanship." Praise quickly turned to anger, however, when the board chairman of U. S. Steel, Roger M. Blough, called on the President April 10 to inform him that the company was raising the price of steel by $6 a ton.

Kennedy denounced the price increase in blunt language at a news conference the next day. He said the Justice Department would investigate antitrust aspects of the case— seven other steel companies had quickly announced price increases in the wake of U. S. Steel's announcement—and the Defense Department would review its steel-buying policies. Administration officials had meanwhile persuaded two steel companies—Inland and Kaiser—to hold their prices unchanged. The eight other companies thus were forced to rescind the increases they had announced. Kennedy had won a victory—but at the cost of incurring the lasting hostility of many businessmen to his administration and the wage-price guideposts. Blough has since spoken of his "occasionally painful" contacts with the guideposts.

EROSION OF GUIDEPOSTS DURING VIET NAM BUILDUP

Business was not alone in its opposition. Unions complained that guideposts bore down harder on wage increases than on other forms of income. The big manufacturing corporations contended that they were watched closely while smaller concerns raised prices with impunity. The AFL-CIO Economic Policy Committee in February 1966 characterized guidepost policy as "an attempt to short-change workers—while there is no guideline for prices and no guideline at all for profits and dividends." Economist Neil H. Jacoby, among others, asserted that guideposts attacked "the symptoms rather than the causes" of inflation and thus "diverted public and official attention from fundamental remedies." [17]

Prices remained relatively stable until the early months of 1965, when the American military buildup in Viet Nam began in earnest. The Johnson administration reacted by exerting new pressure on labor and industry to help hold back rising prices. The government in late 1965, for the first time, threatened to sell metals from its defense stockpiles to bring down prices. Four aluminum producers withdrew a price increase that November after Defense Secretary Robert S. McNamara had announced that 300,000 tons would be sold from the stockpile, enough to glut the market. He later canceled the sale plan. A short time afterward, 200,000 tons of copper were actually sold from the stockpile to ease a copper shortage and keep down prices.

"The evidence of willingness to act," an expert on wage-price policy has written, "is at least as important as the guidepost principle itself." [18] But despite dramatic successes of the Johnson administration in the aluminum and copper "wars," prices continued to edge upward. It was found that

---

[17] Neil H. Jacoby (dean of graduate School of Business, U.C.L.A.), Moskowitz Lectures at School of Commerce, New York University, 1966 (published in *Government Wage-Price Guideposts in the American Economy*, 1967).

[18] John Sheahan, *The Wage-Price Guideposts* (reprinted in condensed form by Joint Economic Committee in record of hearing, Jan. 31, 1968, into wage-price policy, pp. 65-73).

much of the price pressure was coming from food and services—areas not readily affected by the guideposts. It became increasingly hard in 1966 for government to maintain business and labor cooperation. The *Economic Report* of January 1967 omitted any numerical guide for wage increases, and many persons regarded the guideposts as a lost cause.

BRITISH EFFORTS TO HOLD OFF PRICE-INCOME HIKES

Herbert Stein wrote shortly before he was named to President Nixon's Council of Economic Advisers that the "general lesson" of guideposts "is that such efforts either wither away or give way to mandatory controls." [19] The experience of other countries, Stein said, is that the life span of wage-price policies, whether voluntary or enforced, is short.

Among western countries, Britain has struggled hardest in recent years to keep wages and prices in bounds—a necessity in view of that country's shaky economy.[20] The Labor government released a White Paper in February 1965 spelling out plans for a special board to investigate all questions relating to productivity, prices and incomes that were referred to it by the government. The body was established two months later as the National Board for Prices and Incomes. The government had announced that an annual increase in personal incomes of 3 to 3½ per cent would be consistent with the general level of prices, and the board tried to employ "moral suasion" to keep prices and incomes within that limit.

But inflation continued to worsen and in November 1965 the government announced that henceforth it would require four weeks' advance notification of any intent to raise wages or prices. If the government took no action within that time, the increases could go into effect; if the government referred the matter to the board for study, a postponement of two additional months could be required. But the board could only delay—not stop—the increases.

When it appeared that incomes and prices could not be kept in line this way, the government in July 1966 ordered them frozen at existing levels for 12 months. When the freeze order expired in 1967, the board was left with only its old

---

[19] Herbert Stein, "Unemployment, Inflation and Economic Stability," *Agenda for the Nation* (Brookings Institution publication, 1968), p. 285.

[20] See "British Economy Since Devaluation," *E.R.R.*, 1968 Vol. II, pp. 783-801.

powers of postponement and persuasion, and those powers will expire at the end of 1969 unless renewed.

FLAWS IN ANTITRUST ACTION TO CONTROL INFLATION

Some economists advocate strict and broad enforcement of anti-monopoly laws as a means of increasing price competition and reducing inflationary pressures. Others recommend a lowering of barriers to foreign trade and a gradual withdrawal of government price supports for domestic products.

Attorney General John N. Mitchell indicated recently that the Justice Department would enforce antitrust laws vigorously. In a speech at Atlanta on June 6, 1969, Mitchell said that the department "may well oppose any merger among the top 200 manufacturing firms or firms of comparable size in other industries." *Fortune* magazine commented editorially the following month: "Antitrust enforcers will no longer feel it necessary to engage in those tortuous analyses that purport to show how a given merger, because of 'vertical' relations or 'horizontal' overlap of markets, would diminish competition. Henceforth, the Antitrust Division, never noted for acute or diligent research, will be obliged to prove only size."

Antitrust action, free trade and the like may be helpful, especially in combination with other measures, in maintaining price stability. But months or years elapse before antitrust suits are brought to a verdict, and Congress in recent years has shown little enthusiasm for lowering trade barriers or removing price supports. Obviously, other remedies must be sought if the Nixon administration concludes that inflation cannot be starved into submission by monetary and fiscal restraints.

American experience with inflation in past wars suggests that direct controls over wages, prices and such, unpalatable though they may be, are likely to be considered again in the councils of government. Whether Congress can be persuaded to approve direct controls, if asked, probably depends on what happens to prices and interest rates during the remaining months of 1969. If they keep rising, so will the volume of mail from constituents and the pressure to "do something."